EXTRAORDINARY

GUIDANCE

EXTRAORDINARY GUIDANCE

HOW TO CONNECT WITH YOUR SPIRITUAL GUIDES

LIZA M. WIEMER

THREE RIVERS PRESS
NEW YORK

Published by Three Rivers Press, 201 East 50th Street, New York, New York 10022. Member of the Crown Publishing Group.

Random House, Inc. New York, Toronto, London, Sydney, Auckland
http://www.randomhouse.com/

THREE RIVERS PRESS and colophon are trademarks of Crown Publishers, Inc.

Design by Nancy Singer

Printed in the United States of America

Library of Congress Cataloging-in-Publication Data is available upon request.

ISBN 0-609-80060-4

10 9 8 7 6 5 4 3 2 1

First Edition

To my husband, Jim, and my sons,
Justin and Evan

And a special dedication to Grandma Lena and
Grandpa Jack: your unconditional love has been
a guiding force throughout my life.

CONTENTS

ACKNOWLEDGMENTS

My deepest appreciation goes to Peter Occhiogrosso. His outstanding editing and writing skills helped shape my manuscript into the book before you. As with many of the amazing occurrences that led to getting this book published, I have no doubt that I was guided to Peter. We were perfectly matched! Without his talent, devotion, and understanding, this book could not have come to fruition in such a polished manner. Peter, my friend and mentor, I am truly grateful.

Many of my friends, students, and family members have been tremendously supportive during the creation of this book. Their kind words, the stories that they have shared, and their letters have encouraged and taught me so much. From the bottom of my heart, I thank them all. Special mention goes to Dawn Ruminski, Jim Wellman, Lori Bauman, Sarah Kealy, Pamela Lager, Joe and Manuchak Seifert, Kristina Mau, and Mary Wellman (Senior).

My gratitude goes to Leslie Meredith for her vision

and tireless support of this work, and to Sherri Rifkin for her fine editing assistance in helping to shape the final version of the manuscript. And I am grateful to Stuart Krichevsky, my agent, for easing the entire process. No one could have assisted me better.

I am deeply indebted to Betsy Kaplan, whose personal spiritual journey and friendship were an integral part of this book. In the early stages of creating this book I received outstanding editing help from Lynn Wiese and Mary Reilly and many valuable suggestions from Mary Wellman. I will never forget the day Lynn ran out of her office to tell me, "A friend of a friend has a sister who's an editor! I'll get you her number. I have a feeling she'll be the one to publish your book." Sure enough, that's exactly how it happened.

Tom Mahas patiently pointed out areas in my early manuscript that needed work and challenged my thinking. Dr. Robert D. Enright has contributed to healing the world through his research on forgiveness, which has also been of great help to me personally. I am grateful to both of them.

I would like to give special thanks to my sister and friend Heidi Pence, who has truly been a blessing to me. It has been a joy to see her creative success. To my dad, Alan Goldberg, and my stepmom, Cathy Goldberg, who had the courage to follow their hearts and change their life's path, I offer my profound thanks. They inspire their children and grandchildren. And I am grateful beyond words to my son Justin, who wished upon many stars "that Mom's book would get published," to my son Evan, who is too young fully to understand the miracle that he is, and to my husband and soul mate, Jim, who lovingly set aside his projects and ran the household so that I could write this book. Thank you all for your understanding, love, and patience as I strive to fulfill my life's mission.

My deepest gratitude goes to Wil, who has changed my life and in turn has helped me to change the lives of many. And thanks to all the loving spiritual guides who, in their miraculous way, try to help us all make this world a better place.

"We are spiritual guides who have been sent by God to help all individuals realize their spiritual gifts. We provide both practical advice and higher spiritual guidance in the hope that you do not have to suffer needlessly. Be open to our guidance. Let us help you realize your life's purpose."

EXTRAORDINARY

GUIDANCE

CHAPTER 1 ◆

CONNECTION

Like an alarm clock, I heard our four-month-old son, Evan, crying from his crib. It was 2:15 on a windy September morning in 1994. Bleary-eyed, I got out of bed and fed him until he fell asleep in my arms. After I laid him back in his crib, I took a moment to gaze at this little miracle, then crept out of his room. These two o'clock feedings had been my routine for the past month, and nothing appeared to be out of the ordinary. How could I know that momentarily I would embark on a wondrous spiritual journey that would change my life and the lives of many others?

Before returning to bed, I went into the master bathroom. Light shone dimly through the window from a neighbor's lamppost, and all seemed calm. But suddenly I felt an unsettling presence in the room. The sensation was similar to walking down an empty street and having a stranger approach me from behind: eerie, uncomfortable. I looked around. Everything appeared to be in its place, yet I still felt uneasy. I shut off the bathroom light, bolted into our bed, and huddled underneath the covers. My husband, Jim, slept soundly to my right, his back to me. I wanted to snuggle close but knew I might wake him. As I held the covers up to my chin, I felt compelled to look to my left. What I saw left me awestruck.

A bright, shimmering light came toward me in a starburst of yellowish white sparkles. The light source grew until a translucent, exquisitely handsome man's face appeared in its vibrant center. Maybe I should have been frightened, but instead I was elated. His energy overflowed with intense love and kindness. Something deep inside my memory recognized his face. I knew that I was being reunited with an old and dear friend. The name Wil came into my thoughts, and I realized that he was my guardian angel—although he later asked me to use the term *spiritual guide*. I stared at him and thought, You're beautiful! He laughed and smiled, amused at my comment and delighted that I was so pleased to see him.

At the foot of the bed, I saw two smaller light sources. I felt their divine love and sensed that they were present to oversee my conversation with Wil. I call it a conversation, but Wil and I communicated by thought. I heard his words in my head and spoke to him through my thoughts. We communicated simultaneously: before I could even complete a question, the answer would come to me.

Wil began by announcing the reason for his presence. Liza, you have a mission. You are to devote your life to helping people. Do you understand?

"Yes," I responded, even though I had no idea what

"helping people" entailed. Over time, however, my strong faith, combined with the opening of my spiritual connection, would give me the guidance to understand my life's mission. I now know that I am to help others by teaching them to connect with their own spiritual guides in a very easy manner.

As Wil and I communicated, a depressing thought popped unexpectedly into my mind: "suicide." I had no idea where the thought had come from, but as soon as I had it, my body was thrust up off the bed; then, just as quickly, it returned to a resting position. Wil calmly broke through my terror at my lack of control over my thoughts and my body, and said:

> Liza, you are to eliminate all negative thoughts. Negativity will keep you from achieving your life's mission. This was a serious demonstration to show you how damaging negative ideas and influences can be in a person's life. Suicide is the culmination of negative beliefs and surroundings. Unhappiness, unfulfilled dreams, and misery result from negative thoughts. Positive thoughts are as easy to express as negative, if people would only allow themselves to view the world differently. Adversity is not necessarily defeating. Situations that come forth in people's lives will not weigh them down like boulders if they seek positive resolutions. You can help people understand this.

For the first time I clearly recognized how the negativity in my life had been emotionally and physically destructive to me. Wil's comments made sense, and I felt less rattled—although I prayed that my body would never again be hoisted into the air.

In retrospect, I can see that the word *suicide* came into my mind as a reminder of how depressed I had been before I ended my relationship with my verbally and emotionally abusive mother. At times, I had felt hopeless because I believed I had no control over my own life. Through prayer and consultation with my rabbis, I was able to find the courage to change, but where had the notion of suicide come from in the first place?

Around the time I was eight years old, I had a baby-sitter whom I loved dearly. She was fun to be with, compassionate, and creative. But one day, she didn't come to baby-sit, and I later learned that she had killed herself. I saw the horrific heartbreak of her family and how it was quickly silenced by their despair. I, too, dealt with this tragic loss by burying it, although my heart had been torn apart. And yet I realized instinctively that death was not the answer, no matter how difficult life seemed to be. And so began my search for purpose. If life can be filled with despair and yet death is not the answer, then each one of us must have a God-given purpose. Sometimes we need to search through the muck to figure out what it is.

I don't remember why, but Wil briefly left my presence. When he did, I woke my husband. "Jim, guess what?" I said breathlessly. "I just had the most amazing experience. I spoke with my guardian angel, Wil! I've been given a mission to help people! Can you believe it?"

"I believe you," Jim said in his usual nothing-

surprises-me tone, "but let's talk about it in the morning. I'm exhausted." He rolled over and fell back to
sleep. Jim's matter-of-fact reaction didn't upset me. He
had had his share of extraordinary spiritual experiences before we met and believed that people can receive spiritual guidance.

For a few minutes I lay astonished and shaken. I
inched closer to Jim as he slept, hoping to calm my
pounding heart. Once again I felt a strong urge to look
to my left. I turned my head and saw Wil's beautiful
starburst of shimmering light, but without the image of
his handsome face. I noticed that the two other light
sources had returned to the foot of our bed. The anxiety
I'd felt moments before was gone, replaced by peaceful-
ness. I did wonder if Wil had been angered when the
word *suicide* had popped into my mind, and I was still
confused about why it had come to me. "You know I
would never think of killing myself!" I said silently to
Wil. "I don't understand."

> Let me make it very clear, he responded. You misin-
> terpreted my actions. My intention when I hoisted your
> body out of bed was not to frighten you or to express
> anger but to impress upon you the importance of posi-
> tive thoughts. We know you are happy most of the
> time, but you still occasionally allow negativity to over-
> whelm your thoughts. Be positive. You do not need to
> think negatively. Do you understand?

"Yes, I guess I never thought about it before," I said.
Then Wil asked me to restate my mission. Over and

over, these words went through my mind: "I will help others. I will help others."

Wil interrupted my affirmation to say, Well done! Is there anything else you would like to ask?

"Oh, yes," I responded. "Is my father all right?"

After my parents' bitter divorce, my father and I had rarely spent time together, but during the previous ten months he had listened to me discuss my painful relationship with my mother. Now, for the first time since I had become an adult, my dad and I were getting to know each other. The answers poured into my thoughts before I could finish the question.

> Your dad feels guilty because he thinks that somehow he failed his children after he and your mother divorced. His guilt is weighing on his soul, and you can let him know that you forgive him and do not blame him for the past. Now he needs to forgive himself. Tell him he did the best he could under the circumstances. If you relay this message to your father, it will bring him a lot of comfort and relief. Do not worry, your father will be fine.

"I had no idea my father felt this way," I responded.

We talked about my children and husband. Like most mothers, I feared SIDS (sudden infant death syndrome), and Wil reassured me that my baby was safe. He patiently relieved all my concerns and then advised me to nurture my elder son Justin's creative spirit, recommending toys and play activities and suggesting that we buy him puppets. To this day, Justin loves to create elaborate stories using the puppet characters we bought him.

I asked about my friend and neighbor Carin. Wil said, Tell her to renew her faith.

I was puzzled. "What does that mean?" I asked.

Wil's response was clear. Carin will understand. Let her interpret the meaning.

He gave helpful information for other friends along with insights into my relationship with my estranged mother. Wil cheered my decision to remove myself from my volatile relationship with her as wise and courageous. It is not your job to change your mother, he asserted. Let go of the hurt and forgive within your own heart.

"How can I?" I asked. "It's been so hard."

We will help you, he said.

This was the first time Wil had referred to the two other light sources or guides, who had not spoken directly to me. Yet I had been aware that they were communicating with Wil and felt privileged to receive their love and knowledge. Several months after this encounter, these guides introduced themselves to me as Gabriela and Leone and explained their presence. I now know them as two higher guides who have helped me in my life and mission. Their endless patience, love, and sound advice are strong forces in my life.

The dim light of dawn began to peek through our bedroom shades, and my conversation with Wil came to an end at 4:00 A.M. I was exhausted but felt peaceful, loved, and understood. I slept until Jim woke to get ready for work.

As Jim dressed, I lay in bed replaying Wil's messages in my mind, eager to relay them to the appropriate people. I wondered anxiously if the words would be meaningful to my family and friends. After breakfast, Justin and I—carrying Evan in my arms—walked across the street to Carin's home. I needed to know if the message I'd received for her had any significance. As Carin put on her makeup in the bathroom, I sat on her toilet seat and told her about my miraculous experience, leaving nothing out. Finally, I blurted, "I received a message for you."

She dropped her eyeliner and stared at me. I looked straight into her face and said, "Renew your faith." Her expression changed from curious to surprised and slightly shocked. It was obvious that these words had tremendous meaning for her. She confided that she was struggling to merge her present spiritual beliefs, which paralleled mine, with the strict religious teachings of the Roman Catholic Church, in which she'd been raised. She had already confronted this issue when she enrolled her four-year-old in Sunday school, but this message was the catalyst to help Carin talk about her spirituality. Even though it had bothered her for some time, she had never discussed the issue with anyone.

But the message was also significant to Carin because she had been trying for more than a year to get pregnant with her third child. She had conceived her first two children easily and couldn't understand why it was so difficult this time. Immediately after hearing this message, Carin began to examine her unresolved faith. Realizing that it had left a void in her life, she began to define her spirituality for herself and her family. Three weeks later, she conceived her third child, which confirmed for her the importance of having an active faith.

In the afternoon, I called my father, anxious to discover if his message would be equally significant. I was reluctant to tell him about Wil's visit, so I decided to offer another explanation for the disclosure. After a few minutes of small talk, I broached the subject. "Dad, I had a dream about you," I said, "and I was wondering if I could tell you about it."

"Of course," he said. I repeated Wil's words, and when I finished my father confided that he had recently been thinking about the past and felt bad about not having been there for his children after the divorce. He was relieved to hear me say that it was OK, and was grateful for my forgiveness. He was ready to get rid of his guilt and thanked me for the call. "You made my day," he said.

Smiling, I hung up the phone. Once again, the information was right on target. Moreover, that conversation solidified for me the reality of my spiritual encounter. Throughout the day, I had questioned the experience repeatedly in my mind. Had I actually seen and heard Wil, or had I simply imagined the whole thing? But it was too vivid to doubt, and the confirmations from Carin and my father erased any lingering disbelief. I realized that I would never, could never be the same. The information I had received had already begun to have a healing effect on my life and the lives of my loved ones.

Still, in the month that followed, I had difficulty sleeping and always left a light on. Though Wil's visit was a miraculous event, it had shaken me to the core of my soul. As the weeks passed, however, I grew increasingly at ease with the experience and once again felt that I was open, ready, and willing to receive any communication Wil had for me.

After I opened my heart and spirit and accepted the possibility of this extraordinary connection, I started to communicate with Wil regularly. This allowed me to help others with the information he conveyed, which had a tremendously positive impact on their lives. Wil's understanding helped people answer nagging questions and bothersome issues. One woman gained the courage to make the difficult decision to leave her job and pursue her dream of writing and editing. A friend received guidance to help him cope with his aging father's deterioration. Another friend recognized how her difficult past kept her from finding fulfillment in her present relationships.

As those I had helped let others know about the beneficial guidance that was coming through me, more and more people sought my assistance with all sorts of issues. I would ask Wil for advice for them, and I would communicate with their own guides for additional insights. I freely offered my gift to anyone who asked. Yet I felt there had to be more to my mission than providing others with the information I received for them. Though I often thought about the meaning of Wil's statement that my mission is to help people, I never directly asked him what more I was to do with this gift. I strongly believed that the insight would be revealed at the appropriate time. I didn't have long to wait.

One evening my friend Anna came over to receive guidance and to put to rest some questions about her departed father. Amazed at the accurate and helpful information I gave her, Anna chuckled and said, "I wish *I* could get answers from my guides."

I heard her guides reply, "She can learn."

Thrilled, I announced, "I can teach you tonight." She looked at me with disbelief.

"Well, why not?" I said. "After all, I'm a schoolteacher." With Wil's help, I taught Anna how to receive information from her guides. In time she spoke with her departed father, which catalyzed her to renew her faith in God's existence. Anna had been raised as a secular Jew, and although she had attended religious school, God had not been a part of her life. Her experience of connecting with her spiritual guides has allowed her to develop a relationship with God and to reconnect with Judaism.

Spiritual guidance can complement our traditional religious beliefs. Guidance never conflicts with those beliefs. Wil explained to me quite clearly that he and guides like him are messengers of God. In other times and cultures, they have been known by a variety of names and identities, but their function has always been pretty much the same. Eastern religious traditions and folk cultures are rife with spiritual beings who interact with humans on a regular basis. Christians, Jews, and Muslims have all traditionally believed in the role of angels in their lives, although they often conceptualize them differently. One of the most significant examples for Christians was the Archangel Gabriel announcing to Mary that she would be the mother of the Son of God. Many Roman Catholics and Protestants believe that each of us has a guardian angel who helps us make the right decisions in life and protects us from some kinds of danger.

Jews have many ideas about angels. The Hebrew Bible speaks frequently of figures called *Malachim,* or divine messengers, including figures who drove Adam and Eve from the Garden of Eden, stayed Abraham's hand when he was about to sacrifice his son Isaac, wrestled with Jacob, and assisted the prophets. In medieval Judaism, it was not uncommon for Kabbalistic scholars to receive guidance from a *maggid,* or discarnate spirit, while asleep or awake. Joseph Caro, the sixteenth-century author of the *Shulhan Arukh,* the most authoritative code of Jewish law for Orthodox Jewry, claimed to receive much of his information in nightly revelations from a heavenly figure embodying the *Mishnah.* So, too, did the Vilna Gaon, who lived in the eighteenth century and is considered by many to have possessed the most brilliant mind ever to study the Torah.

In recent decades, we have seen an astonishing increase in the number of personal accounts of angelic intervention in the lives of ordinary people. Similarly, many contemporary scholars and authors have once again embraced the possibility of connection with the spiritual world on many levels. Opening to that world is what this book is all about.

Just as I've learned to communicate with Wil and other spiritual guides and avail myself of their loving wisdom, you can develop the ability to connect with your guides. Doing so will help you work through practical problems and difficulties and help others by acting compassionately and spreading the wisdom your guides offer you. Your guides can give you complex spiritual insights as well as advice on more mundane issues. Never overlook or underestimate the value of practical advice from your guides. From major events like marriage or divorce, the birth of a child or the death of a loved one, to the more commonplace occasions of everyday life, your guides can help you avoid needless suffering. The fact that we may learn through suffering doesn't mean that we have to suffer to learn. Just being stuck in a dead-end job or an abusive relationship isn't necessarily going to help you grow spiritually. If your guides can help you move on by suggesting something as practical as a new job or new response to an old pattern, they will be doing you an enormous service.

After I taught Anna how to communicate with her guides, I understood that my mission was to reach out to other people who are seeking spiritual guidance and teach them this remarkable gift. I began to offer evening workshops for people who wanted to learn to communicate with their guides and departed loved ones. Most of those who came to me had no prior experience with receiving guidance outside traditional religious instruction. They had different religious backgrounds and degrees of faith, but they all seemed to grow spiritually. Spiritual guidance helped my students feel a stronger connection with their faith and with God, as well as an increased connection to other people, a virtue recognized by all the great religions as compassion.

Wil provided me with the questions, answers, and simple, step-by-step instructions by which I conducted these workshops. He also explained a process for dealing with what he called "barrier issues." Barriers are states of mind or predispositions that prevent us from receiving spiritual guidance and achieving our goals. (I'll say more about them in Chapter 9.) All of Wil's instruction is contained in this book. He explained:

> It is not necessary for people to meditate or use incense, candles, crystals, certain music, or specific words for connection to occur. Communication with spiritual guides is for anyone who is open, ready, and willing to begin this helpful and often miraculous journey. Spiritual background or prior "experiences" are not needed to converse with your guides.

It is not necessary to conceive of spiritual guidance as coming only from external guides. We also learn to hear our own inner voice of guidance, which some call the Higher Self or the embodiment of our highest wisdom. I think of the Higher Self as the God part of us, our soul, the most profound aspect of our nature—what in Hebrew is called the *nefesh*. When we connect with it, we gain self-knowledge. Although the techniques taught in this book will help you connect with your innermost self and develop your intuitive nature, they are intended primarily to help you connect with your spiritual guides, which are clearly something else. Our guides convey information, advice, and insights that we could not possibly know on our own. Becoming better acquainted with your Higher Self is a form of spiritual guidance, but your Higher Self is not the same as a spiritual guide no matter what form your guides assume. No matter how your guides communicate with you, whether through images or hearing, through clear articulation or just a feeling or sense, they can help you discover more about who you are and what your innermost strengths and weaknesses are. Your guides will help you become more yourself.

Wil's advice will allow you to connect with your guides for the first time and to strengthen connections you have already formed. It will help you make positive changes in your own life and assist others with their life issues. When you picked up this book, you took the first step toward opening your heart and mind for communication with your guides. As you read further, you will discover the mechanics of that communication. You will learn to determine, for instance, whether your principal mode of communication is visual (seeing), auditory (hearing), or kinesthetic (feeling), and how to communicate with your guides in each of these modes. You may find that you receive messages in a combination of modes; I get most of mine auditorily, but sometimes I'll see an image or get a strong physical or emotional sensation. You will learn the basic guidelines for communication as well as how to overcome the major barriers to connection and avoid the most common mistakes and misperceptions about connecting with your guides.

Many of the people I have taught have been amazed that they received answers to the very first questions they asked. They were even more surprised at how simple the process is and elated that they could connect anywhere, anytime. A few individuals had to work through a barrier issue before they could connect, but once they resolved it, they were able to communicate with their guides. Be patient with yourself as you embark on this remarkable journey. Know that your guides are always with you, ready and willing to offer their help. They want you to discover your purpose, and, in time, you will.

CHAPTER 2 ◆

WIL'S MESSAGE TO
THE READER

Welcome! Your spiritual guides are excited to have the opportunity to communicate with you. We have been with you for a long time, some from before your birth. We see your joys and sorrows with an unconditional love for you. We never judge your actions; we strive to help you become a better human being and fulfill your life's mission. We come from God's divine light, to guide, teach, watch, instill values, and build your faith in a Higher Power. In our eyes, it is unimportant who you were; we care about who you are and who you will become.

When you receive spiritual guidance, you are being connected to a different state of consciousness. Different states of consciousness can mean your subconscious, your instincts, your soul, and even dreams of or contact with departed loved ones. Since death is merely a transition to a different level of energy vibration, departed souls can be thought of as different states of consciousness that, under the proper circumstances, you may be able to contact. Even coincidence or fate is contact with another consciousness state. The "Higher Self," the soul or part of each person linked to God, is also a consciousness state—a spiritual consciousness state. When you communicate with your spiritual guides, you connect with a consciousness state that is in the spiritual realm.

Every living thing has an energy, a spirit, or a state of consciousness that belongs to God. Even something you might find despicably ugly contains beauty because it is a part of God and of the universal balance. That is why caring for other human beings as well as for the environment and God's creatures is necessary.

We do not use the term *angel,* although some people call us by this name. The term *spiritual guide* encompasses all spiritual beings whose purpose is to guide and teach God's unconditional love. Even departed relatives can be spiritual guides, but most have not reached the state of unconditional love and knowledge that your own guides have attained. We are messengers of God, fulfilling our duties to God. Just as you strive to do God's work on earth, we strive to assist you in every way we can to help you accomplish what God expects of you. Know that no person's purpose is deemed less meaningful, necessary, or important than any other's.

I have been with Liza since long before she was born. I understand what she is meant to accomplish in her life, and I watch and guide her with unconditional love. I never interfere with her free will to choose her own path. Your guides will act in the same fashion. Liza's life has not been an easy one, but her trials and tribulations are typical of many who walk the earth. Like most, she continues to learn and grow. As part of Liza's life mission, we have asked her to write this book, knowing that many will be able to identify with her.

The purpose of this book is to teach you to connect with your guides in a simple, step-by-step manner. We will examine day-to-day issues and how your spiritual guides lovingly help you. We want you to see yourself in the examples we provide and know that you, too, can receive daily guidance that will make your life more beautiful and less complicated. Your guidance will depend on your needs and God's will. Most of your communications will be with a guide who has been with you for a long time. Rejoice, for this guide understands you well and is thrilled with the opportunity to help you. God bless you, and go in peace.

CHAPTER 3 ◆

MY BACK PAGES

For you to make the most of the practice of receiving spiritual guidance that you will learn in this book, it will help for you to know the key issues and questions in your life. Most of us tend to get so bogged down in the day-to-day activities of survival that we need to step aside sometimes and look at where we are and where we want to go. If we don't take the time to examine our lives, we run the risk of perpetuating old patterns without ever breaking free and giving ourselves the chance to move on and live fully.

One way you can determine your key issues and challenges is to write down a brief outline of your life history. Concentrate on the turning points in your young, middle, and later years—no matter how old you are. You might begin by asking yourself how you would most broadly characterize your family of origin. How do/did your parents interact with each other, your siblings, you? What would a good relationship with them look like? What do you need to say or do to make yourself whole?

I had begun a similar process of life review shortly before Wil appeared to me, and I continued to go through it for some time afterward. Although what I saw wasn't especially pleasant, examining my life helped me to clear away some of the blocks in my past and get ready to move on. So let me tell you a bit more about myself so you can see that, painful as my past has been, your life may have some similarities to mine, since my issues are not dissimilar from many people's. Even if your experiences and mine are different, we share the ability to connect with a higher or inner source of spiritual guidance.

I am an ordinary housewife from Milwaukee, a part-time religious-school teacher, a hopeless romantic, and a die-hard Packers fan, yet I've decided to devote my life to teaching people to receive spiritual guidance. Before Wil appeared to me, I would have thought that such a thing could happen only to Shirley MacLaine or someone who is deeply religious. I didn't think anyone would believe my story or listen to what I have to say. Yet nothing happens in a vacuum, and Wil's appearance was the culmination of a long and painful struggle within my heart and soul. Looking back on the turning points in my life after he spoke to me that chilly September morning, I began to see that the path I'd followed wasn't so random after all. Everything seemed destined to move me along to the next step I needed to take.

The one thread I saw connecting all the events of

my life, the one belief that has sustained me throughout, is my knowledge that God exists. Before I had words to express this belief, I knew that I had come from a higher Source; it was just something that I understood deep in my soul. Because I felt God's loving presence, the act of praying always came naturally to me. I communicated with God on a regular basis, not in a formal way but by sharing my deepest thoughts and feelings. Although answers to my questions often came to me, I was never consciously aware that I was receiving spiritual guidance. Only after Wil and I started communicating on a regular basis did I realize that I had been guided throughout my entire life, and that he had been helping me all along to prepare for my mission.

I began to understand, for instance, that Wil and I had conversed long before that September morning. I recalled memories that I had previously dismissed as "just a child's creative imagination." Sometime before I was five, I had my first experience of a shimmering light that appeared in the middle of the night, surrounding my bed and then departing. For several weeks when I was five years old, I saw starbursts floating above my bed. Terrified at first, I would huddle under my covers and beg the squiggling lights to go away. And they did. But on each succeeding night, they appeared above my head until one night I decided to ask what "they" wanted. I had decided to make friends with the lights, thinking that if we became friends I could stop being scared. This may have been the logic of a five-year-old, but it worked. Wil spoke to me then.

We are here to watch over you, he said. *Do not be frightened, our dear child of God. You are safe.*

Even though you may not have any such specific memory of a guide "intervening" in your life, if you look closely at your childhood, you may be able to recall moments when a sense of God's presence or the guidance of one of God's messengers filled your heart. At the time you may not have had the words to express what this presence was, but you will probably be able to bring those moments to mind now. It may have been something as simple as the beauty of a natural scene—a magical winter snowfall or the first time you woke up early enough to see dew still clinging to the grass. It may have been a kind word from someone just when your fragile world seemed about to fall apart, or an apparent coincidence that with hindsight you view as a small miracle.

I had been praying to God to answer one very difficult question. I wanted to know why I had been born to the family I was in. My mother was extremely strict, and I felt as if I didn't belong. Wil answered my question, and although I'm not sure I was totally pleased with the response, I accepted it. *Liza*, he replied, *often you cannot understand why you are going through something, but someday you will. Know that you are always safe and that you are loved by God. We are with you.*

These words are my last memory of speaking directly with Wil until he reappeared in my life. His words, however, remained vivid in my mind even as I minimized their source to conform to logic. In times of despair, I would softly repeat his words to myself: "Someday I will understand."

If there are questions that once haunted you, try to recall them and write them down. Don't overlook questions about the religious beliefs and practices that you were brought up with and that, for better or worse, have molded the way you think and interact with the world. Were your parents devout, casual about their faith, nonobservant, agnostic, or completely atheistic? Do you feel that their beliefs were genuine or superficial, something they lived by every day or just for social propriety? Ask yourself how you feel about the belief system they passed on to you. Is it something you would like to explore more deeply?

Even if doing so makes you profoundly uncomfortable, I recommend that you try to immerse yourself in your birth religion to seek the answers you've been looking for. Talk to religious leaders until you find an individual and community with whom you feel comfortable. You cannot make a good decision about a spiritual path unless you have achieved a basic understanding of your own faith through study and worship. If you have extensively asked questions and searched for meaning in your faith and have not found spiritual fulfillment, then examine other belief systems. Whatever faith you choose, it's important for you to feel at home.

I grew up in a Conservative Jewish household in a suburb of Milwaukee where very few Jews lived. We kept Kosher, celebrated the Sabbath, and observed the holidays. My parents were active in a number of Jewish organizations, and my mother was a professional volunteer who set an outstanding example by supporting causes that she believed in deeply. Yet entrenched as I was in the Jewish way of life, being a Jew was something I felt I needed to hide. I wasn't ashamed of being Jewish, but I sensed the danger that came with my faith. Anti-Semitism was prevalent, and with the Nazi rallies in places like Skokie, Illinois, just eighty miles from where we lived, and later the near annihilation of the Israeli team at the 1972 Olympics, I began to fear that I, too, might be destroyed because of my faith. My mother, who was born in this country during World War II, instilled in my sister, my brother, and me that each of us was living for one of the six million Jews who had died in the Holocaust. My life and my soul belonged to one of them, and my mother made it clear that if we failed to live as faithful Jews, it would be as if we had destroyed not one life but two: our own and that of the Holocaust victim. I embraced this awesome responsibility by reading as many books on the subject as I could find, but the weight of all that suffering only made me feel more alone.

Though my faith had already had a strong impact on my life, it became even more important to me as my world began to tumble around me. The day before I entered seventh grade, my parents announced that they were getting a divorce. The next few years were chaotic and painful and only through the grace of God did I endure the bitterness between my mother and father and the disturbing loss of our family life. In retrospect, I can see that my feeling out of place in my family was just a reflection of the imbalance in the family as a whole; my discomfort was part of my parents' discomfort with their marriage.

In examining the traumatic moments in your own life, you may be able to see them now in a larger context—to see, as I can, that all the participants in your drama were suffering in different ways. Once you view things from this perspective, you can begin to let go of the anger and resentment that come from believing you were singled out by the universe for abuse while those who caused your suffering somehow escaped.

Certainly my mother endured her share of pain, but it became clear to me that her actions and attitudes strongly contributed to the events that caused her so much distress. Unfortunately, she couldn't see this, despite some tremendous losses in her life. Soon after the divorce, her own mother disowned her, her sisters stopped speaking to her, and my older sister and younger brother moved out. As more and more people exited our lives, my mother spoke constantly of being victimized by those she loved, and I was too close to her to believe differently. I remained fiercely loyal to her, even though her actions toward me were abusively controlling and manipulative.

During these difficult times, I would often sit alone and pray. Talking to God was a source of strength and the way I was able to cope with all the challenges that surfaced between my mother and me. I was determined to endure what life had in store. My newfound conviction was put to the test the summer before my freshman year in high school, when I personally encountered religious bigotry for the first time. My mom had remarried and, that summer, she and my stepdad rented a permanent campsite on a lake, where I soon met other kids my age. But one day, the idyllic splendor of those summer weekends by the lake was shattered when one of the boys I'd met blurted out, "Heil Hitler! Kill the Jews!"

Slightly nervous, I retorted, "Then you'll want to kill me."

"Why?" he asked.

"Because I'm a Jew!"

The boy looked at me with shock and embarrassment. "But I thought Jews had horns," he said, with what looked like genuine amazement. "I've never met a Jew before."

"Until now," I said smiling.

Over time, I came to realize that he had spoken from ignorance rather than hatred; as we got to know each other, his attitudes changed and I was able to forge a friendship with him. At the same time, I recognized that I could no longer live in fear of being a Jew, and that I could counter ignorance before it turned into the poison of hatred.

If you look honestly at your own life, you may be able to discern similar moments when you were able to transform ignorance or confusion—your own or others'—into wisdom, friendship, or harmony. As you examine such events, ask yourself if it's possible that you were receiving guidance without realizing it. You may even have asked for God's help in a moment of panic or despair, and then, after the crisis passed and the dust settled, you may have forgotten that God answered you.

In high school, my conflicts with my mother continued to escalate. When I accepted a homecoming date with a boy who wasn't Jewish, she accused me of wanting to murder one of the six million all over again and grounded me for three months. During that time, at my mother's insistence, I reluctantly accepted an invitation to join a Jewish youth group. Unexpectedly, the group turned out to be a source of great joy for me. I developed rewarding friendships with my peers and found an outlet for my spirituality. I buried myself in the activities of the group, where I studied Torah and participated in social action and charitable activities. The comfort and connectedness of being able to study, pray, and socialize in an organization devoted to building Jewish identity and repairing the world through social activism was exactly what my soul craved. Now I see that I was being guided to explore my religious roots more deeply than I might have consciously desired at the time. I'm glad I did.

Illnesses and physical problems, either permanent or chronic, can be great indicators of crucial developments in our lives. Take a closer look at any ailments or painful symptoms that you have now or have overcome. Do you feel that your physical problems are or were related to the events of your past? Can you let go of those traumas as a way of healing your ailments and moving on? If not, what is keeping you from letting go of them? Often we don't even realize the connection between disease and its underlying causes, which may be psychological, emotional, or spiritual.

The summer before I entered college, I met my future husband, Jim—a tall, handsome, blond-haired and blue-eyed gentile. I don't need to describe my mother's reaction when she discovered that I was dating him. Although she accepted Jim after he chose to convert to Judaism before we became engaged, my relationship with her continued to be strained.

Shortly after my mother found out about my relationship with Jim, I began to suffer severely from an affliction that was eventually diagnosed as Crohn's disease. I experienced searing abdominal pain and was barely able to keep food down. I endured bout after bout, occasionally needing hospitalization to get the symptoms under control. Looking back now, it seems incredible that I didn't spot the connection immediately, but it was eight years before I realized that my symptoms were brought on by my inability to cope with my mother. After each horrible argument with her, I would have another bout with the disease.

Once again, however, this apparently debilitating development led me to the next step in my spiritual evolution. Eighteen months after my first son was born, I had surgery for a bowel obstruction caused by inflammation from Crohn's disease. I spent four weeks in the hospital, at times gravely ill. A kind older man peeked into my room on a day that I could barely get out of bed. "How are you doing?" he asked.

"OK," I responded.

"I'm a volunteer from my church," he said. "I go

around and help to cheer people up and pray with them if they like." He paused. "Would you like me to pray with you?"

"Sure," I said hesitantly.

He came in and sat next to my bed. He asked me my faith, and I told him that I was Jewish. "God will listen to our prayers," he responded. Taking my hands in his, he prayed with me, and I felt strength from his touch. Though I have no idea who this man was, I am certain that he was a catalyst for my recovery. By the next day, I had started to improve greatly. Ten months after my surgery, I became pregnant with my second son, but my joy was quickly deflated when the doctor found a large mass on my ovary. After several ultrasound tests, the doctor told me that I would need surgery. Again I turned to prayer, telling God that this was too much for me to bear. Although I didn't know it then, a close friend was praying to God using the same words. Two days later I had another ultrasound, which showed the mass had almost completely disappeared. In my mind this was nothing short of a miracle. This time I immediately got the connection between prayer and healing, and it planted firmly in my heart the importance of prayer as the foundation of my life.

Look at the moments in your life when a seeming chance occurrence, sudden impulse, or apparent coincidence led to a major change in direction. See if it isn't possible that you were being guided without your conscious knowledge. The turning point in my life came when I found the courage to break off my relationship with my mother. On Yom Kippur, the Day of Atonement and the holiest day of the Jewish year, she told me that I was a terrible daughter. When I asked her why she would say that, she said, "This is how I feel. You can't change how I feel." I was coming to the realization that it was my choice to continue or to let go of what was clearly an abusive relationship, but I hesitated to act on my belief. I prayed for guidance.

Then, on an impulse, I called my sister. The two of us had barely spoken during the past fifteen years, and my voice quavered as I asked her why she had left home. I was astonished to hear that she had endured much of the same treatment I had. Somehow that conversation provided the impetus I needed to call my mother and inform her that I would no longer see her. Hanging up the phone, I felt a great sense of freedom and relief. Taking back control of my life began a healing process in my soul and body. It has taken me quite some time and a lot of inner work to forgive my mother, but I have, and the rewards have been immeasurable. Since that time, I've had absolutely no symptoms of Crohn's disease.

My decision to stop being a victim also opened the door for my connection with Wil. A little more than ten months after I separated from my mother, Wil appeared. He proved his declaration years before that someday I would understand why I was born into my family. My mom, dad, stepparents and other relatives, and everything I've accomplished and even suffered through have all helped me become the person I am today.

Try to determine the most significant turning point

in your own life. Can you discern the hand of guidance there? What have been your best life decisions? What do you believe inspired them? Do you have any regrets?

If the thought of writing down all the personal information you've gathered while reading this chapter seems overwhelming, you may want to consider another approach. If you're visually inclined (a distinction we'll explore shortly), you may find it appealing to create a chart of your life using paints or colored pencils. Draw the major events from each of the key years in your life and write in how they made you feel. Graph the ups and downs in your life. Is there a recurring pattern—for instance, is every big high followed by a corresponding down period? Can you discern an overall trend up or down? What can you do to move the chart in the direction you would prefer?

If you are more comfortable with the spoken word, you might tell your story into a tape recorder; pretend you are recounting your life to a valued friend or counselor. Then listen to the tape as if you were that friend or counselor. What interpretations and advice would you offer the person on the tape?

If you're more kinesthetic, or feeling-oriented, you may want to reenact in front of the mirror key scenes from your life and examine the feelings they evoke in you. Don't dwell on just one event, but explore what happened before and after to try to get an overview of your most common experiences and emotions. Imagine how you might feel better freed from old negative emotions and how you might experience happy emotions more often.

Gaining this kind of perspective on your life will help you open the inner doors of perception and pinpoint the areas that need to have more light shed on them. Your guides are ready to help you, and being open to their guidance can lead you to a new understanding.

CHAPTER 4

PREPARING TO CONNECT WITH YOUR SPIRITUAL GUIDES

You may wonder why it's necessary to prepare for spiritual connection, since Wil arrived in my life without any apparent effort or preparation on my part. The explanation is fairly simple. In a sense, I had been preparing for connection even though I had not been aware of doing so. In looking back on the year before Wil's early morning visit, I realize that many extraordinary things had happened to me that I cannot easily dismiss as coincidence. I can attribute these occurrences only to divine guidance, because logic alone cannot provide credible explanations. Although my preparation was unconscious, you can prepare yourself in specific ways so that you may receive guidance consciously.

Before beginning Wil's instructions, however, I want to emphasize that communicating with your guides is not about seeing starbursts of light and feeling ecstatic, although these things may happen. It is about maximizing your ability to help yourself, others, and the world. The experience of connection may be quite pleasant, but think of that pleasure as an incidental by-product. The point of connection is larger and more profound than the experience itself.

Although you can receive guidance without asking for it, learning to communicate with your guides and consciously seek their assistance can have a tremendous impact on how you view yourself and the world. From personal experience and from teaching others to communicate with their guides, I can assure you that preparing for connection is not a complicated or taxing process. You need only three simple methods to get started:

1. Make time for prayer in your life.
2. Examine prior experiences to determine whether they can be attributed to divine guidance.
3. Form the desire to connect with your guides.

I'm convinced that my constant faith in God and my daily prayer life helped open my heart and mind to the possibility of having spiritual guides. The Bible is filled with stories of angelic intervention and divinely guided experiences, so I knew that such interaction was possible. Since I already believed that I was being watched

over on some level, Wil's visit wasn't a complete sur-
prise to me. Many people have asked me if their guides
will appear to them in the middle of the night as Wil
did. I tell them that this is highly unlikely. Wil made it
very clear that the purpose of his visit was to get my attention so that I could help people become aware of
their own guides and communicate with them. If such a
specific role had not been selected for me, I know that
Wil would not have been so dramatic.

DEVELOP A PRAYER LIFE

Daily prayer does not have to be formally structured as
it is taught in religious schools or practiced in formal
religious institutions. You can pray to God in a heart-
felt, individual way. For as long as I can remember, I
have had conversations with God through prayer. When
I pray, I offer thanks and praise for the blessings I've
received, express concern for family and friends, and
ask for help with problems that I feel are difficult to understand or hard to bear. I also pray in the tradition of
my Jewish faith by saying the *Sh'ma* (*Sh'ma Yisra'el,
Adonai Eloheinu, Adonai, Ekhad.* "Hear, O Israel, the
Lord is our God, the Lord is One"). I attend a syna-
gogue and recite prayers with my family at home. In
whatever tradition you were raised or currently practice, regularly communing with God is the fuel that
keeps the flame of faith burning. If you feel that the
early training in prayer you received in your birth religion was mechanical or inadequate, or if you feel un-

comfortable creating your own prayers, read some of
the excellent books that have appeared recently pre-
scribing deeper and more contemplative approaches to
prayer, for instance, Larry Dossey's *Prayer Is Good
Medicine* or *How I Pray,* edited by Jim Castelli.

Although prayer is a very effective way to prepare
for connection, connecting with your guides is no sub-
stitute for prayer. We do not pray to our guides, although, as God's messengers, they may convey God's
answers to us in some form. The following example illustrates how prayer can open the door to guidance. A
close friend named Beth told me how sad she felt after
deciding not to fly home to visit her family. Having recently given birth to her third child, she hated the
thought of her family not getting to meet her newborn
son. But she and her husband had examined their financial situation and reluctantly agreed that the trip
was impractical. With a heavy heart, she told me how
she planned to pray for the ability to live with this decision. "Pray to accept this for now," I said, "but ask God
to help you find a solution."

Although she could not imagine an answer short of
winning the lottery, she agreed to give this approach a
try. A few weeks later, her mother called and said that
she wanted to reimburse Beth for the frequent flyer
ticket Beth had sent her earlier that summer. At first
Beth refused her mother's offer because the ticket had
been a gift. After thinking about it for several days,
however, she realized that her mother's offer had been
the answer to her prayer. Beth called her mother to ask
if her offer was still open and if she could use the money

to purchase a plane ticket to fly home. Delighted, her mom agreed. A month later, Beth took her youngest child on his first plane ride "home."

INCREASE YOUR AWARENESS OF GUIDANCE

Apart from prayer, one of the best ways of preparing yourself for spiritual connection is increasing your awareness of guided experiences. You can do this by identifying situations that you believed were coincidences. You will usually find that they actually were not. Of course, some coincidences are just that and have no perceptible meaning, but when "coincidences" begin to accumulate and direct your attention to a certain person or event, it is wise to pay attention and look for a discernible pattern.

Have you ever received a call from a friend shortly after you thought about him? If you can accept the possibility that the two of you tuned in to each other in some fashion, then consider communicating with your guides along similar lines, by "tuning" your consciousness to align with theirs. Think back over those times in your life—whether they were momentous or seemingly mundane—when things appeared to happen miraculously. Maybe a last-minute change of plans took you to a different restaurant, where you ran into an old friend and rekindled that friendship. Our lives are often filled with such simple occurrences that we somehow overlook.

I've experienced plenty of these "chance meetings" or synchronistic events myself, and even though connection has become a natural part of my life, I am still astonished by them. One took place on a spring morning a couple of years ago as Jim and I prepared for our first vacation alone in three years. The anxiety of leaving Justin and Evan overshadowed my excitement about the trip. What ifs invaded my thoughts. What if there is an emergency? What if the kids wear out Jim's mother? What if I can't bear to be separated from them? The list continued to grow as I dropped Justin at preschool and ran my last-minute errands. After I'd made three unsuccessful attempts to find blue shoe polish, Wil suggested a store around the corner that was not on my morning agenda. When I pulled into the parking lot, I saw my friend Anna leaving the store. She took one look at me and asked, "What's wrong?"

"I don't know if we should go on this trip," I replied. "I'm worried about the kids." I ran down my litany of doubts, but Anna's reassuring words eased each of my concerns and completely changed my mood. I gave Anna a hug and entered the store feeling relieved and once again excited about the trip. When I saw that the bin for blue shoe polish was empty, I understood that the real reason Wil had directed me there was to receive a little comfort from an old friend.

As your spiritual awareness becomes stronger, so will your ability to notice and utilize the opportunities that present themselves in your life. If you sense that you are meant to go somewhere, call someone, or do something that is not dangerous or harmful, I encourage you to act on that feeling and see what happens. Take heed of any uncomfortable feelings, however, and think about your options before you decide to proceed. A sudden impulse to go skydiving for the first time or to explore that fascinating cave you passed while walking along the shore needs to be weighed a lot more carefully than a strong but inexplicable notion to see a new play when you've never had the urge to see one before. You may waste some money and time if the play turns out to be a bomb, but you're unlikely to sustain a serious injury.

People sometimes ask whether our guides actually create or lead us into dangerous or difficult situations to help us learn by suffering. Absolutely not. Bad things do not happen because our guides want us to "learn a lesson." Bad things happen not because of anything we have or haven't done but because billions of other people are also exerting their own free will. Our guides watch over us and try to keep us from harm, but events will occur that challenge us physically, emotionally, and spiritually. Regardless of the situation, if we have the ability to think, we can find options available to us. Sometimes, though, we need assistance to see things a little differently or see other, less obvious options. Our guides and prayer can help us.

For most of my life, I saw myself as a victim who was powerless to control any aspect of my life, especially my relationship with my mother. Once I recognized that I had the choice whether or not to remain in that relationship, I gained the courage to distance myself from her. Spiritual guidance provided insight and helped me to take charge of my own life. Such guidance can help us cope with the ramifications and emotional fallout of adversity we have faced in the past. It also can help us grow in the present to prepare ourselves for the future. If you are currently struggling with personal or spiritual issues and are seeking answers, you are ready to connect with your guides.

The events in our lives are like building blocks: each block represents a different emotional, physical, or spiritual experience. Childhood traumas can sometimes make the building blocks of early experience fragile and the base on which we try to build the rest of our lives shaky. Our guides can help us identify problems and patch up our faulty suppositions so that we can build stronger lives. Because my mother and I had a very unsteady relationship, my base for future relationships, security, and health was weak. As our interactions became increasingly strained, I would easily fall apart with each argument. I hadn't learned to cope with past pains, to reshape my faulty reactions. Once I broke away so that I could reexamine my life and reshape my foundation, my life became stable again.

HAVE THE DESIRE AND INTENTION TO CONNECT

Along with prayer and an increased awareness of subtle connections and guided experiences, you must sincerely want communication from your guides. Your desire to receive answers from them, however, must not replace your ability to make your own choices. You should not turn over your personal power to your guides. Instead, use their assistance to enhance your judgment, discrimination, and effectiveness. I do not ask questions of my guides just for the sake of asking, nor do I spend my days having private conversations with Wil as the world passes by. When I'm playing with my children, watching a movie, sharing a private moment with my husband, or chatting with friends, I almost never communicate with my guides. Days and even weeks can pass without an "eventful" connection.

Still, there are times when I receive information regardless of whether I have asked a question. That raises the issue of whether information received spontaneously represents a message from a guide or is intuition or memory, or just a passing thought. To begin with, once you open yourself to connection with your guides, the channels stay open, especially if you continue to work at being open. In certain situations, your guides may provide you with information they feel you need to know even though you haven't asked. This isn't common at first, but it tends to happen more often once you have established regular communication with your guides through practice and a conscious decision to be open.

In fact, as we learn to connect with our spiritual guides on a regular basis, our ability to tune in to our own inner knowing, our Higher Self, also increases. All of our spiritual senses, including intuition and ability to visualize, become heightened as a result of opening the channels of communication with our spiritual guides. A woman I had taught to connect told me that while on a retreat she noticed someone who seemed to be especially quiet. It wasn't clear why this woman was so detached, so my student asked her guides for any information that might help her understand the situation. She received a message that the woman was under a tremendous burden that she needed to unload. When the time was right, she would unburden herself and my student should be prepared to be loving and supportive. Within the next few hours, the woman revealed tearfully that her husband was extremely ill and had told her not to tell anyone, but that now she needed to share her pain and concern. My student's guides helped her be better prepared to deal with a situation she couldn't have known fully through intuition alone.

Even though I try to remain alert to guidance, when I have not asked for information directly sometimes I can dismiss it as "just" a passing thought. More often than not I misread messages received while performing mundane tasks. We must learn to pay attention as much of the time as possible. For example, one day I wanted to pick up the dry cleaning before the babysitter had to go home. I was running late and was certain that my purse was in the car. After arriving at the dry cleaner's, I realized that I had left my purse at home. It hit me that during the ride there I had dismissed the passing "thought" that my purse was at home on the counter. Instead of paying attention to this thought or checking around the car for the bag, I dismissed the thought by reassuring myself that my purse was in the backseat. I drove home smiling at my own obtuseness and arrived to find my purse on the counter. Whether this was an unsolicited message from Wil, trying to save me some valuable time, or just intuition is probably less important than the fact that I chose to ignore the thought. I've since learned to be more attentive to any inner stirrings.

Although you may have the strong desire to connect at this point in your life and your guides are ready to communicate with you, do not feel pressured to connect with them until you are ready emotionally, psychologically, and spiritually. It is perfectly acceptable to wait until you are at ease with the idea of connection. You may first need to address one of the barrier issues that can interfere with your ability to communicate with your guides (see Chapter 9). One day, for instance, a friend's guides informed me that she was ready to communicate directly with them. For months I had been receiving helpful guidance for her and her husband, and though she knew that I taught connection, she had hesitated to ask me to teach her how to communicate. Three months after I relayed her guides' message that she was ready to communicate, she asked me. She had needed time to understand the process and extinguish her fears.

Although I have explained how prayer and awareness of guided experiences can help you prepare to connect with your spiritual guides, do not be alarmed if prayer hasn't been a part of your daily life or you can think of only a few guided events. If you are ready to receive loving guidance, your spiritual guides will be there for you, and the method taught in this book will help open the lines of communication with them.

CHAPTER 5 ◆

HOW DO I KNOW IF I AM IN CONTACT WITH MY SPIRITUAL GUIDES?

When you first try to connect with your spiritual guides, it is natural to question whether you have really received a message from them. You may feel that you're just making up the answer or reflecting your own thoughts. You may even feel that what you are hearing, seeing, or feeling is coming from your Higher Self or, in other terms, your own soul. Sometimes it can be difficult to recognize this difference. But realize that your spiritual guides can give you information that you could not possibly discern on your own.

To begin to distinguish the sources of the information you receive, ask yourself, "Was I thinking when I wrote this answer?" You will most likely know the truth. If you are still unsure, ask yourself, "Is the information insightful? Helpful? What I expected?" At times your guides' message will confirm your thoughts or feelings on a particular question. You can surmise whether this information actually came to you from your guides by asking yourself if you were able to set aside your preconceived notions and allow the information to flow to you. Just because your guides confirm something you already believe, however, does not mean that you did not receive guidance from them. But if you ask ten questions and each answer reflects your beliefs, it's a good idea to stop. Ask over and over until you have a strong yes or no, "Is this answer coming from my guides?" If you hear a no, which would indicate that the answers are your own, ask your guides, "Is there anything else about _____ that I need to know?"

Don't dismiss your beliefs; they have value and importance. But if you stop with them, you may miss a helpful perspective. So, to get past your own ideas, link questions together. Sometimes the first answer you receive can reflect your own thoughts. That's fine, but continue asking questions that will help open the flow of communication between you and your guides. The following exchange illustrates this point.

QUESTION: What do I need to know to help Randy at school?

ANSWER: Randy has to take responsibility for his actions. He must recognize situations in which he gets angry and lashes out at other students. He can find a more productive way to handle his anger and frustration.

RESPONSE: This could have come from my thoughts.

I know Randy has had difficulty controlling his frustration.

This is a situation in which your guides can reflect what you already know. But keep going. Ask the next logical question, for which you yourself may not have a preconceived answer.

QUESTION: How can I help Randy find a more productive way to handle his anger and frustration?

ANSWER: Randy is a good child. He doesn't always realize that his actions hurt others until it is too late. Take some time to act out with him both his and the other child's feelings. Try to control your own frustration when you see him failing to meet your expectations. You love him! Your irritation only agitates the situation.

RESPONSE: I didn't realize my frustration could be adding to the problem.

QUESTION: What can I do to cope with my frustration over his behavior?

ANSWER: Acknowledge it.

RESPONSE: What does that mean?

ANSWER: You've been very angry at his behavior, and then you yell at him for being bad. But you've never stopped to reflect past your own anger. You lash out with your anger and frustration without taking a moment to step back and look for other solutions.

RESPONSE: I didn't realize my reactions were so unproductive!

ANSWER: It's OK for Randy to know you're angry. But it's time to move beyond the anger. We will help you.

The first message reflects the woman's thoughts and could have come from within. But as she continued to ask questions, the answers helped her to recognize a different issue. Privately, she explained to me that she had expected an easy solution to her question, but the answer helped her realize that the problem was much more complex. Her guides later provided insight into her behavior and Randy's, and in turn she was able to help him.

Another way to recognize a message from your guides is to review how you received the message. When I receive answers for others, I sometimes hear phrases that they use frequently but I don't. For example, I was teaching someone to connect when I suddenly heard her guide say, "Y-E-A-A-H-H!" in a very enthusiastic and drawn-out way. I could not remember the last time I'd said that, so I asked her, "Do you say 'Yeah!' a lot?"

"All the time," she told me, "as a way to encourage my children."

Her guides had communicated to me the same way she speaks to others. That was a pretty clear sign that I had received the message from her guides.

Yet many students who have connected for other class participants have also told me, "I know the information was not from my own thoughts, because the message was so different from the way I would have answered."

For some, the response to a question was so loud and clear that it was as if they were speaking with a friend over the telephone. For others, especially those who received visual images, communication with their guides was less obvious. However, when they thought about the image's meaning or shared it with the person who asked the question, it proved helpful and insightful.

For example, in one workshop, Andrea asked how she could cope with stress. A classmate, Clara, saw an image of a cardboard box being removed from a space. When it was time for Clara to share the message, she hesitated. She could not imagine any correlation between a cardboard box and eliminating stress. Yet she told of the image anyhow, and Andrea explained that it was quite significant. Stacked in her basement she had cardboard boxes filled with paperwork that needed to be filed. For several months she had procrastinated, and now Andrea realized that she could unload some stress if she finished filing the documents.

A sense of calm, peace, and well-being can be another sign that you are in contact with your spiritual guides. You may feel relaxed and deeply focused. Sometimes, when I listen for a message for a person who is in the same room, I focus on something other than the individual. I am always aware of what is around me, but this technique helps me to concentrate on what I am to receive.

Trust and faith are important factors when you determine whether you have actually connected with your guides. Without faith and some amount of trust, connection will be very difficult, if not impossible. As you practice and receive helpful information for yourself and others, any doubts you have will begin to fade. It is also perfectly natural for you to experience physical signs of connection, such as tingling or chills. One person I know gets a tingling sensation in her scalp and will run her fingers through her hair in response. Or your body may be engulfed in a pleasant, warm feeling. Another student knew she had connected because her tongue pushed to the roof of her mouth whenever she received a yes answer to a question. When I started to communicate with Wil, my index finger flickered upward whenever I received a yes answer. Though these responses may seem strange, they are helpful and can be an accurate sign of connection. After you have been connecting for a while, your sign will most likely go away. Though you may miss the sensation, rest assured that you are still connecting with your guides.

Keep in mind that your guides may contact you without any initiative on your part, as Wil sometimes does with me. You may hear their message in your thoughts or receive a visual image even if you do not consciously try to connect. One day, for example, my husband received a message from his guides to drive carefully to avoid an accident. As he drove to work, a car followed him closely. Remembering his guides' words, he slowed down to put more distance between his vehicle and the car in front of him. He had a feeling that the space ahead of him would be crucial in avoiding an accident. Suddenly, an auto cut in front of the vehicle tailgating Jim. This set off a chain reaction causing the drivers in back of Jim to smash into one another. Jim accelerated to avoid being rear-ended by the car that had cut in behind him. Jim had no doubt that his guides had provided this information to keep him safe.

I have often received information to go somewhere, call someone, or do something that I never would have thought about doing on my own. Since the "instructions" were so out of the ordinary, I knew that they must have come from my guides. Each time I followed this type of message, the experience was a learning opportunity for me and sometimes even for the person or people I encountered. If you feel uncomfortable with what you are guided to do, you have the choice not to do it. But if you are able to follow your guides' message, do so. A meaningful experience will most likely come out of it. Early one morning, I received a visionary message. I saw myself at a nearby park, standing on a concrete patio overlooking the water. An older gentleman approached me from behind on my left side. I was told that if I spoke with him, he would help me resolve an issue.

I decided to see if this would happen, so later that morning I went to the spot in the vision. As I stood on the balcony overlooking the water, an older gentleman walked over to me. There he was, exactly as expected, yet I was surprised. Did I dare tell him about the message? We smiled at each other, and he asked, "Why are you standing all alone?"

"Just taking a break," I said, "enjoying the scenery and thinking."

"What's a young lady like you have to think about?" he asked. "You don't have marriage trouble, do you?"

"No, my marriage is great," I responded. "Actually, I believe a friend is upset with me. Whenever I ask her about it, she says everything is fine. But I know something is wrong. So that's why I'm here, to get the answer."

"Is she a good friend?" he asked.

"Oh, yes."

"Well, then," he said confidently, "call her up. Ask her to lunch, and tell her straight out that you know something is wrong. You'll talk about it and then you'll be done with it. You'll continue as you always did."

"Thank you," I said. "I'll definitely follow your advice."

And I did. That evening, I went to my friend's home to watch *Sisters*. I shared the entire experience with her; then I came right out and asked her what was wrong. "Well, I didn't know how to approach you," she said, "but I've felt that you need to be more assertive and take some time for yourself once in a while. You're never away from the kids."

I laughed. "And I was worried it was something serious," I said. Yet I knew she was right. I needed to give myself permission to go out once in a while and leave the kids home with Dad. This remarkable guided experience made me aware of how our guides can provide opportunities for personal growth.

Frequently, people in my workshops ask me if a negative spirit will try to communicate with them. Maybe it's a residue of the fear that we all live with, or perhaps just an indication of how Western religions have traditionally denigrated attempts at contacting spirits. It seems to be all right for angels to contact *us,* but we are made to feel that our own attempts to contact spiritual beings will result in an encounter with evil. I have on rare occasions met mischievous or deluded spirits, which often turn out to be the souls of departed relatives (not necessarily mine!), but such disturbing connections are the exception. Be assured that your guides are present for one purpose and one purpose only, to help you help yourself, others, and the world. There is a simple and foolproof way of determining whether you are receiving messages from a negative spirit.

Wil has said,

Though negative streams of consciousness exist, we, your spiritual guides, want to stress clearly that you should not be concerned or fear them. If for any reason you hear or see anything that you perceive as negative, you must ask yourself if the information reflects a negative belief you may have about yourself. You are specifically asking to connect with guides who come forth to you out of love and light, so there really is no question of negative guides interfering.

Sometimes, when you feel uneasy, a departed soul will come to you to pass on a message to you or to a loved one still on earth. These occurrences are extremely rare and should not be a concern.

If, however, you still have any feelings of uneasiness, then say to yourself, "I am safe and secure and surrounded by God's light," and envision this. Know that you are always in control. If you are at all uncertain about whether the spirit is positive, simply ask, "Do you come forth out of love and light?" Your question must be directly answered with a yes or no. Nothing else is acceptable, since universal law requires that the truth be given to you. If the answer is no or you are unsure, firmly demand that the negative spirit leave your presence immediately and never return. It must depart. This, too, is universal law. You have nothing to fear.

If any uncomfortable feelings linger after such an experience, seek the help of your guides, sing a hymn, or recite a prayer, according to your preference. Say, for instance, "I belong to God" (or Jesus, or Allah, or the Buddha), sing or listen to "Amazing Grace," or recite the *Sh'ma*. This will serve as a source of strength and a reminder of the Higher Power that is the Source of all connection. But keep in mind that the uncomfortable feelings are most likely projections of your own fear, and you ought not let fear prevent you from seeking guidance.

People also often ask about the possibility of communicating with departed loved ones and whether they can be spiritual guides. Wil explained,

It is possible for you to communicate with deceased individuals. Simply ask to speak with a particular soul out of love and light. Your loved ones will communicate with you if they are able to do so, which is not always the case. But keep in mind that conversing with deceased individuals can be a much different experience from communicating with your guides. Your loved ones will have opinions and can express themselves in both a positive and a negative manner.

Departed loved ones of individuals with whom I have close contact often come to me to pass on messages. I can sense their presence and get information from them. I am always in control, however, and can choose to allow the communication to end. If you feel uncomfortable, say so and ask the spirit to leave at once. Seek the help of your guides if necessary.

Now that you have seen examples of how your guides will communicate with you, it will be easier to separate your thoughts from your guides' messages. As you receive your first several messages from your guides, pay attention to physical signs, the tone of the information, and how you feel. These things can help you gain confidence in your ability to communicate with your guides. Remember, only through practice will you be able to develop this gift to its fullest potential.

CHAPTER 6 ◆

THE THREE MODES OF COMMUNICATION

As the mother of two small boys, I have very little personal time. So, if communicating with my guides was complicated or time-consuming, I wouldn't be able to do it. Knowing that you have plenty of responsibilities, too, I teach a process of connecting that is simple and accessible. You don't need to study for years with a master or learn complex meditative techniques. All you really need is the belief that connection is possible, the desire to learn, and the willingness to spend as little as ten minutes a day practicing the few fairly simple methods you'll find in this book. To begin with, though, you'll need to determine which of three common modes of communication is your dominant one.

Wil conveyed the following information to explain the ways individuals connect with their guides:

Spiritual connection can be accomplished in many ways. We can appear in "light" form and even in a physical form. We can guide you to do something in such a way that you will do it without knowing why. You may get a sense that you are to proceed in a certain direction or take action, and you have a clear choice whether or not to proceed. You may also use spiritual materials, such as candles, incense, or crystals, to help you connect. Deep meditation, yoga, and prayer are other ways to be in contact with us.

What is taught in this book is different from these techniques. Still, you may want to explore these and other avenues to bring a special balance into your life. Though this is a diverse list, there certainly are other ways we in the spiritual realm can communicate with you. We ask you to seek balance in the physical, emotional, and spiritual essence of your being. We can align with anyone who is open to connection by using the very simple method taught in this book. Your guides' sole purpose in coming forward now and in this way is to reach out to you and help you to fulfill your life's purpose.

The method taught in this book uses three modes of communication. When you communicate with your spiritual guides, you will receive your answers in one or more of these modes: *auditory* (hearing), *visual* (seeing), and *kinesthetic* (feeling). Wil explained:

Communication by thought is tuning in to a different frequency, just like changing a channel on the TV or radio. You cannot see microwaves or radio waves, but you know they exist. These energies, as well as others, are a part of your daily life. With spiritual connection, the brain waves that receive communicative information will align with our frequency. The information transmitted will vibrate at a rate that will enable you to receive the message from us. When you are in tune with us, you will receive our messages by hearing, seeing, or feeling what we convey to you. Know that by whichever method you receive the information, you can trust it is our answer to you.

Although I receive most of my own messages auditorily, on occasion I'll receive them visually or kinesthetically. Sometimes I may feel a person's physical symptoms. For instance, a woman once walked into my house and I immediately felt light-headed and had to sit down. I asked her if she felt faint, and she said that she did and had been diagnosed with diabetes. Whatever the mode of communication, you'll need to understand the difference between your own thoughts and information from your guides. When you think about something, the thoughts come from within you; they are your own ideas and beliefs. When you receive information from your guides, you must first clear your mind of your own impressions and thoughts about an issue.

You may hear, see, or feel the information from your guides. You may receive information in all three modes. If you hear messages from your guides, the experience may be like listening to an audiocassette for the first time. Write down everything you hear as you hear it. Do not be overly concerned about comprehension as you write. After you have finished, go back and read for content. (I'll discuss more detailed guidelines for keeping a journal in the next chapter.)

For auditory communicators, the information you receive may be so strong that you will know you are actually hearing a separate voice. At other times, the information comes within your thoughts, though the "voice" of this wisdom is quite different from your own. The distinction between your own thoughts and the voice you hear in your thoughts may at first be rather subtle. You may want to observe how you silently talk to yourself to help you differentiate your thinking from what you may eventually hear in your thoughts from your guides. What do you sound like? When you speak about yourself, for instance, you most likely use the word *I*. When your guides communicate with you auditorily, they will say *you* or your name.

Sometimes messages will come to you in the form of images of words or pictures. If you receive mental images, the experience may be similar to watching a silent movie. First describe or draw the images in your journal, then go back to decipher their meaning.

Finally, the messages may be in the form of feelings. People who become very emotional when they hear a story, regardless of the content, respond to information through their feelings. You may have been told as a child, "You are too sensitive." In terms of communication, however, "sensitivity" is precisely how these people react to information. Because kinesthetic responses are the hardest to explain, a couple of examples may help. After pairing two participants named Ally and

Ronna in one of my courses to practice receiving guidance for each other, I noticed that Ronna had become very emotional. Tears were streaming down her cheeks. Ronna said, "I don't know why, but when I started to ask about Ally's question, I couldn't stop the tears from flowing."

The question ("What does Ally need to know about work?") had nothing in it that should have caused such a response, so I asked Ronna to explain what she was feeling. "I just feel so sad and frightened," she said, "but I don't understand it."

After Ronna took a few deep breaths, she asked her guides why she felt so sad. Her internal kinesthetic response was then followed by a surprising image. "I see Ally driving a white truck. I also see a danger sign, as if something might be harmful to her. I don't understand it."

Ally did. She explained that she worked for a delivery service and drove a white truck. The danger sign had to do with the chemicals that she sometimes transported. The sadness Ronna felt directly reflected how Ally viewed her job and how uncomfortable she felt with the dangerous chemicals. Ronna received reassuring information that Ally wasn't in any immediate danger, but that she might want to look for a job that would give her more satisfaction and peace of mind.

In another seminar, Ben asked his partner, Carolyn, what he needed to know about his father. Suddenly Carolyn's stomach started to bother her. She asked her guides why she felt this way and realized that Ben's dad had stomach problems. When Ben confirmed this,

Carolyn's external kinesthetic response disappeared as quickly as it had come. With additional guidance, it was apparent that Ben's father was ignoring his symptoms and that Ben could help his dad by encouraging him to seek treatment.

Now that you are aware of the different ways you may receive information, the next step is to determine your preferred communication style. People process information differently, and once they establish their method of communication, they can follow the instructions for connection that will be most beneficial to them. These modes of communication are the same ones used to receive information from your guides: *auditory, visual,* and *kinesthetic.*

The following lists of statements will help you determine what style of communication best suits you. You are an *auditory communicator* if you agree with most of the following statements.

1. I prefer to hear instructions.
2. If I am lost and stop to get directions, I easily follow verbal instructions and rarely need to write them down.
3. Information becomes clearer when I hear it.
4. I easily comprehend verbal information given in a lecture.
5. When asked to spell a word aloud, I easily complete the task without writing or visualizing.

You are a *visual communicator* if you agree with most of the following statements.

1. I prefer to see instructions.
2. If I am lost and stop to get directions, I visualize where I am to go or need to look at a map.
3. Information becomes clearer when I read it.
4. When I listen to a lecture, I comprehend more if I see the information on lecture notes, slides, chalkboards, and so on.
5. When asked to spell a word aloud, I first visualize it in my mind.

You are a *kinesthetic communicator* if you agree with most of the following statements.

1. I prefer to learn by doing instead of listening to instructions or reading directions.
2. If I am lost and stop to get directions, I prefer to draw a map to help me get to my destination.
3. Information becomes clearer when I am allowed to "do it" instead of just hearing or seeing it.
4. When I interact with others, I tend to feel what they feel. For example, when someone is sad, I feel sad. If someone is cut, I may feel the person's pain.
5. When asked to spell a word aloud, I need to write it down first.

Once you decide which style of communication fits you, follow the instructions that apply to your choice. If you are unsure or can relate to a combination of the communication modes, read each one and proceed with the instructions that you believe best suit you.

Your guides will communicate with you in the same

way you communicate with others or in the manner that pleases you the most. If you are direct and to the point when you speak to others, you will most likely receive your information in this way. One woman I've taught enjoys word games. Her guides know this and sometimes give her messages alliteratively—through words that begin with the same letter. One time she counted twenty-two words starting with the letter *s* in a message. Her guides also know she loves to learn new vocabulary, so she sometimes needs a dictionary because she is unfamiliar with a word in the message. Whether you prefer poetry or short, direct answers, your guides will communicate in the manner that suits you best because this is the easiest way for them to align with your energy.

When you start to connect, you may receive one-word answers. Do not be concerned about this. You can comprehend plenty from one word. Continue to ask your questions and the answers will begin to flow. Remember, the content of the message is more important than its length.

If you find it difficult to communicate with your guides, do not give up. Ask yourself if a fear or some other issue is blocking your ability to connect. An effective way to alleviate your fears is to say the following affirmation: "I am open, ready, and willing to communicate with my spiritual guides. When I communicate with my guides, I am safe, secure, and surrounded by love."

If one set of instructions does not work for you, try another, or combine two. Even though you follow the instructions for your preferred communication style, you may still receive information from your guides in another mode. For example, visual communicators may periodically hear or feel the information their guides communicate to them.

Now that you understand how your guides can communicate with you, you are ready to begin the procedures Wil gave me for receiving spiritual guidance. These guidelines are outlined in the next chapter, which explains the important principles to follow in the process of communicating with your guides.

CHAPTER 7

GUIDELINES

Shortly after I taught Anna, my first student, to connect with her spiritual guides, Wil provided me with a list of directions that would help all my students. At first the list had little meaning for me, but over several months a number of situations arose that helped me recognize the significance of each of his points. I also came to realize that the directions, which he called "guidelines," are not hard-and-fast rules. In fact, I've broken every one of them at one time or another. As I did, I became aware of how each guideline provides structure and parameters that can help us connect more easily. Some are just suggestions for simplifying the process; others may help preserve your integrity and well-being; still others relate to common courtesy.

If you fail to observe a guideline, the gift of connection will not be taken away from you. It is always very important, however, to do your best to follow each one. In this way, receiving guidance will become a natural occurrence in your life. Each guideline has its own merit; one is not more important than another. After you read and understand each one, agree to follow it to the best of your ability. (See Appendix 1 for a list of the guidelines.)

1. KEEP A JOURNAL.

Choose a notebook or journal of some kind and use it exclusively for writing down your questions and the information you receive from your guides. If you have determined that your dominant mode of communication is visual, you may want to consider getting a journal with blank rather than lined pages to make it easier to draw the images that come to you. In any case, it's easier to convey accurately messages intended for others if you write them down as soon as you receive them. A journal will also prove valuable when you need to refer back to past messages.

One day I wrote down a message for an out-of-town friend who was having a crisis of faith. He had lost his mother two years before, and now his father was dying. Over the past few years, he had also left his birth religion (Roman Catholicism) and had explored other traditions, but he had not really made a commitment to a new practice and felt at sea spiritually. He had stopped praying and having any relationship with God, although he retained some general spiritual beliefs. The message I received was that he needed to reconnect with his belief in God and to restart his prayer life, regardless of whether he rejoined the church.

Shortly after, I called and read him the message. He responded that he had been pondering that very issue only an hour before. Grateful for the insight, he said he would think about his relationship to God in more specific terms. Six months later when he came to visit, however, I received new information on the same issue, so I went back to the previous message and reread it to him. He decided to look at the question even more closely.

Writing in a journal provides an excellent opportunity to see themes or patterns in your messages. If you notice a theme or pattern, ask yourself what it means. You might be able to identify a barrier to connection or your spiritual growth or a personal habit that you may want to alter—or amplify. Whatever it is, your guides will be delighted when you notice it.

Obviously, it is not always possible or convenient to write down the information you receive, especially if you're driving, sitting in a business meeting, or doing the dishes. If you want to write a message down, ask your guides to wait until pen and paper are accessible. Ideally, of course, you could work on improving your memory, but sometimes the messages can be so complex that I don't feel comfortable recommending this approach. Again, your guides will help you develop the best way for receiving information.

2. BE A CLEAR AND DIRECT COMMUNICATOR.

Clearly and carefully write down exactly what you hear, see, or feel as soon as you receive it. Then read what you've written and think about its meaning. If you don't write down your messages immediately, your own judgments, interpretations, attitudes, and faulty short-term memory can prevent you from communicating the information correctly. The same thing can happen if you hear a message but alter it slightly to fit your preconceptions. An acquaintance of mine named Ellen once asked if I would help her coworker Sara resolve questions about her father's recent and sudden death. As I talked with Sara on the telephone, her guides told me that her father had died in his mid-fifties. Although I heard this information, I dismissed it. This can't be correct, I thought. Ellen is in her forties, and if Sara is the same age, then Sara's father must have been older than that. So I asked Sara if her father had died in his mid-sixties. "No," she said. "He was fifty-six."

"Well, how old are you?" I asked. She was twenty-nine. This experience reinforced for me the importance of being a clear and direct communicator and not putting my own "beliefs" into the information given me. Always strive to give a precise translation and be aware of your assumptions.

3. IF IN DOUBT, ASK FOR CONFIRMATION OF WHAT YOU RECEIVED.

If you are unsure that you received the information correctly, ask your guides to confirm the message. Write in your journal, "Is the information I wrote regarding _____ correct? Yes or no? Do I understand your message clearly?" If you still doubt the answer's accuracy, wait awhile and ask the question again. A woman I had taught tried to decide whether she should retire. She asked her guides and thought she received a yes, but she was not positive. She then asked, "Did I receive the correct answer?" She saw a visual image of the word *no*. She repeated her question and saw *no* again. When she asked "Why not?" she was given a list of unforeseen reasons. The final decision to retire, however, was hers to make. As it happened, she decided not to retire. Since she doubted her first response, confirmation was crucial for her to identify a clear, accurate message.

4. SPEAK THE TRUTH.

This is clearly a guideline to follow all the time, not just when you communicate with your guides, but it is particularly important for connection. Speaking the truth can be difficult, especially when it may hurt a person's feelings. In a lot of life situations, it can be more compassionate not to speak a truth. You must be truthful, however, when someone asks for your opinion regarding a message. Express yourself in a kind, loving way so the information is helpful rather than hurtful. If you feel that you may be bringing your own critical judgment or lack of acceptance to the message, then you must say nothing, even if what you have to say is true. Truth must be balanced with kindness and love.

A member of one of my workshops related a story to me that illustrates the danger of placing truth over compassion. He had been participating in a holistic health fair when he observed a woman asking a channeler to provide her with insight about her relationship with her husband. The channeler blurted out, "Your husband is having an affair with a younger woman."

The recipient of this distressing information sat in stunned silence for a few moments, then began to cry uncontrollably. The channeler later bragged about the accuracy of her message, telling others how the woman had carried on. This kind of behavior calls into question the integrity of the channeler's intent to use the gift of connection to help others. The woman who broke down in tears may have known the information was true, may have merely feared as much, or may have been caught completely off guard. Recognize that your actions and words must reflect not only truth but also compassion.

Sometimes we try to get out of uncomfortable situations with a white lie. We have all turned down invitations with made-up excuses. Most people know when they are being lied to, however, so take a moment to reflect on how you have felt when someone lied to you.

These apparently minor incidents can influence your ability to trust others and to be trusted. Telling the truth is a habit, and the more you break the habit, the easier it becomes. If you are able to rectify a situation in which you acted dishonestly, then do so. One time I returned a gift to a store at which it hadn't been purchased but which I knew carried the same product. The owner asked if the merchandise had been purchased at his store. At first I said yes, then I said that I didn't know. In other words, I lied. Even though I exchanged the item for a similar one of lesser value, I knew I got what I wanted through a lie and it bothered me. First thing the next morning, I went back to the store and told the truth. I offered to take back the item I had exchanged. The owner told me that it was OK and added that he was very appreciative that I had returned to talk to him about it. He gave me a certificate for a free cup of coffee and told me to come back again.

In retrospect, I see that this was as much a matter of balance as of telling the truth. The owner may have known I was lying and chosen to go along so that he would not lose a potential customer, but he probably hadn't felt very good about the whole episode. My owning up not only helped me but may also have helped him put the incident behind him and get back in balance with the universe.

5. IF YOU RECEIVE INFORMATION ABOUT SOMEONE AND YOU ARE UNSURE WHETHER YOU SHOULD REVEAL IT, ALWAYS ASK. IF YOU FEEL UNCOMFORTABLE WITH THE INFORMATION, DO NOT REPEAT IT. YOU HAVE THE RIGHT TO CHOOSE WHAT YOU SHARE.

It is very important to proceed cautiously with any information you receive that could disturb another's well-being. Ask yourself and your guides, "What will I accomplish by revealing this message?" If you choose to proceed, it is best to take an approach that allows the person to reveal the information to you rather than to deliver "disturbing" news. In most circumstances, the person for whom you received the information already has some knowledge of it but may not have discussed it with anyone. Make sure you examine all the possible consequences of revealing a disturbing message, in case the person for whom it was intended chooses to discuss her situation with you. Remember, the only reason you receive confidential information is to help. Any other motivation to divulge a message is unjustifiable.

I once received news from Wil about some major trust issues in the marriage of a friend. This was not something she had ever discussed with me, so I couldn't verify it, and I proceeded cautiously. Each time I saw or talked with her, I casually asked, "Is everything OK?" When she replied that everything was fine or changed the subject, I didn't press her. But after several months passed, I decided to pursue the issue. "Are you sure you're OK?" I asked emphatically.

The question made her defensive. "Do you think something is wrong?" she snapped.

"Well," I said hesitantly, "I sensed things weren't right, but I'm glad everything's fine." The subject quickly changed, and I let the question drop. Four months after I received the disturbing disclosure, my friend confirmed what I already knew. It had been difficult for her to admit to herself that her marriage was in trouble. But Wil's message had prepared me, and I was able to give her the love and support she needed.

6. REMEMBER THAT INFORMATION IS CONFIDENTIAL.

Like Guideline 4, this one applies to more than just spiritual connection. We are often tempted to pass on information we have about others that, although true, serves no good purpose and can actually cause harm. People sometimes say that gossiping isn't wrong if the information is true, but that doesn't make good spiritual sense. The same thing applies to information you receive from your guides. If you believe the information should be shared with someone other than the parties involved, ask their permission and that of your guides. Do not turn the information into the latest gossip, even when the situation appears auspicious or you see no harm in passing it along. Always respect the person's privacy if he or she refuses your request.

One evening while I was discussing connection at an acquaintance's home, my hostess mentioned the name of a person I knew casually. As I began to recount an experience that involved him and my family, I distinctly heard Wil tell me that it was unnecessary to reveal my saga. But since I'd started, I felt I should complete the story, so I ignored his advice. After I finished telling the tale, the mood changed subtly yet noticeably. Everyone seemed a bit deflated. While I was driving home, Wil gave me a few reasons why it was unnecessary to repeat my gossip, even though the conversation was not based on a message from my guides. First, although what I had to say was truthful, it was not very nice. Furthermore, the words I spoke did not benefit anyone but only brought out painful feelings. And, finally, the whole story put a damper on a wonderful evening. Wil expressed no anger or judgment, only a kind, insightful response. When I expressed my regret, he said, There is no way to change your decision now. But the next time a situation like this comes up, remember this experience and do not repeat it.

7. UNDERSTAND THAT CONNECTION IS A GIFT.

It bears repeating that the only reason to connect with your spiritual guides is to improve and help yourself, others, and the world. When you ask a question, it must come from your heart. If you need to clarify your question's purpose, ask yourself, "How will this information help me or others?" When a message changes the life of another person in a positive way, you will understand why connection is a wonderful gift. With your guides' help, you can provide the answers for a person who is struggling to make a decision, is stuck on a certain problem, or needs encouragement to follow his or her spiritual path.

Recently, a woman who took my workshop wrote to tell me that because of the guided information she received, she and her fiancé are pursuing their dream careers. She had asked the class to help her obtain information on her career path. The answers referred to working with the elderly in a hospice setting. Astonished, she stated that she had always wanted to work with the elderly. Once she made the decision to pursue this path, the information she needed poured in from all around her. It confirmed for her that she is on the right spiritual course.

Though connection is extremely helpful for receiving the answers you seek, do not use it as a means to solve others' problems without their permission or request. Doing so constitutes meddling in their business. Instead, be open and ready to receive a helpful message for someone even though you did not specifically ask for it. Do not question or interpret its meaning. Write it down and, at the appropriate time, share the message with that person. If he or she asks where you obtained your information and you feel uncomfortable discussing connection, state that you believe it was inspired by

God. You will be telling the truth. Remember, it is always your choice to disclose information.

Late one night as I lay in bed, relaxed but unable to sleep, I suddenly heard a message for a coworker who was trying to make a decision about a job offer. I got out of bed and, under a night-light, wrote the message down for her. The note addressed obstacles, rewards, and her ability to inspire others. When I read it to her the next day, she could not believe how accurately the words described her situation. The message helped her decide to take the job. Though she has since had conflicts, her job change and the positive influence she has exerted have proven tremendously rewarding for her and the people with whom she now works. To this day, she carries the note in her purse.

8. CONNECTION IS TO BE USED FOR SPIRITUAL GROWTH. USE WHAT IS REVEALED TO YOU ONLY FOR GOOD, OUT OF DEEP LOVE, TO HELP YOURSELF, OTHERS, AND THE WORLD.

When you begin to communicate with your guides, knowing that connection is used only for good, a wonderful transformation takes place. You become more conscious of your judgments, your life improves, and you gain a better understanding of yourself and the environment in which you live. You will also be more aware that you—and all around you—are part of one universe. Do not charge for information you receive unless your guides say to do so. It is quite appropriate, however, to utilize information from your guides to improve your skills or gain insights that create business and personal opportunities.

Thomas came to one of my workshops contemplating a job change. He had been at his current job for more than nine years, felt comfortable there, and knew what to expect, although he had begun to feel he needed to make a change in his life. A week before the workshop, however, an opportunity had arisen for him to interview at a company with which he had dealt regularly for six years. He knew and enjoyed working with a number of key people there but was still unsure about making the switch. Thomas later revealed that, while any major change is hard for him, this decision was particularly stressful because there were so many uncertainties about the new position. He feels most confident with a precise job description but wouldn't have that because the position had just been created, and he had to make a quick decision, without knowing exactly what to expect. Given my instructions, he asked a very general question of his partner, who had no inkling what a momentous decision this was for Thomas.

QUESTION: What does Thomas need to know?

ANSWER: Slow down, your mind is racing. Stop, think, and then pursue. Ask questions. Go for it! There is an older man you admire, a mentor. He will help you.

THOMAS'S RESPONSE: "I had been thinking a lot about the job and had been asking myself a lot of questions, but the 'go for it' provided the confidence I needed. The mentor was an older gentleman who had offered me the position. I had known him for the past six years and admired him. This message confirmed for me that he would be the trainer and motivator I needed at this time in my life. I took the job, and it has been everything I could have hoped for. Although I'm paid about the same as before, I work fewer hours and see a better future ahead. I'm truly grateful!"

9. BE PATIENT WITH YOURSELF AND OTHERS.

This is another guideline worth following all the time, not just when you connect with your guides. Being patient with yourself and others means that in situations that would normally cause you distress, you choose to react calmly. When you sense that your tolerance is ebbing, take some deep breaths. If this doesn't work, try to take a break or remove yourself from the stressful situation until you regain control. As a friend and I talked one day about how difficult it is to be patient with our children, I asked her what happens when she starts to yell out of frustration and anger. "The situation intensifies," she said, "and my child may react with defiance and become more out of control, which infuriates me even more."

I then asked her what happens when she reacts patiently in situations that would normally make her irate. "I'm able to reason with my child and resolve the problem more quickly," she said. "I'm most successful when I get down on my knees, at his eye level, and calmly and firmly explain what is and is not acceptable behavior."

When my tolerance is low for a particular situation, I may take a moment to ask my guides for help. If I can't clear my mind enough to receive the answer, I may say a brief prayer, something like this: "Dear God, I am so frustrated and angry right now. Please help me be more patient." When I calm down, I am able to ask my guides for insight if I have not successfully resolved the issue myself. A helpful observation from your guides can turn frustration into relief and understanding. Your guides have a limitless ability to be patient with you. They will not interfere with your free will but will wait until you are open to their guidance.

Connection also requires a certain amount of patience. For some, communication with their guides will come quickly, but for others it can be a slow process. When you do connect, you may not always understand the message immediately. Be patient. Most likely it is meant for you to decipher sometime in the future. Put it aside, knowing that eventually you will know what it means.

From time to time, you may have difficulty receiving a needed answer from your guides. In these situations, you may have to wait or discover the answer yourself. Your guides cannot remove your personal responsibility to make decisions and take action. They are like parents who say to a child, "It is time for you to take responsibility for your choices." Sometimes your guides' lack of response is meant to provide you with the opportunity to seek your own answers through actual experiences. This does not mean that your guides are abandoning you. Just be patient and ask for their guidance, love, and protection while you proceed on your journey. Be open to learn, realizing that when you are patient you will be better equipped to attain your goals.

10. FORGIVE YOURSELF AND OTHERS FOR SHORTCOMINGS. WORK ON YOUR OWN IMPROVEMENTS.

This guideline appears to be simple, yet when was the last time you let yourself off the hook for something? We have all done things we regret, but if you still replay the same story or events in your mind, then take some time to ask yourself why. Do you really want to continue to punish yourself or the other person or people? Each time you relive the injustice in your mind without resolution, you bury your happiness in anger, misery, and pain. Forgiveness can give you the peace you seek. But it's one thing to say "I forgive you" and rationalize that you no longer need to be angry. It's another thing to feel that forgiveness in your heart. Ask yourself if your heart has held on to the pain even though your head has spoken the words of forgiveness. When your heart is able to say, "I no longer need to feel the pain from this experience," you can release the pain and move forward. Love yourself for who you are and be open to new possibilities. Finally, let go of the baggage of your past, start to live in the present, and allow yourself to believe that your future can be terrific. Letting go is never easy, but here are some simple suggestions based on my own experience, readings, and guidance from Wil.

1. Acknowledge that the event in question has caused you a tremendous amount of pain. Don't bury the event; bring it to the surface and confront it. Allow yourself to feel the anger or hurt it arouses. You can acknowledge the event in any or all of the three modes in which you communicate with your guides: auditorily (by talking about it), visually (by writing or drawing), or kinesthetically (by acting it out).

2. Ask yourself if you really want to stay angry or frustrated. Holding on to your anger will not hurt the people who may have been involved in the event, but it will hurt you and the ones you love. It may be time to say, "I can't do anything about this because it's in the past. What I *can* control is how I look at the situation today." If so, then it's also time to let go of the event, whether it was something you did or something that was done to you.

3. Plan your next step. If, for example, you've been laid off from your job, sit down and make a list of all your skills. Then make a list of your dreams, both past and present. Based on those two lists, what kinds of realistic goals can you set for yourself? And, finally, how will you go about realizing those goals? Be as concrete and specific as possible.

In a lecture entitled "Educating for Forgiveness," Professor Robert D. Enright of the University of Wisconsin, Madison, explained, "When you forgive, you know there was an injustice against you, but you now choose a different response. You understand that the wrongdoer must be held to a higher moral standard, and though the individual has no right to ask for compassion, you give it nonetheless."

Professor Enright emphasized that forgiveness is a choice. "It is a journey that may take a great deal of time. In addition, forgiveness and reconciliation are not one and the same. You do not always reconcile when you forgive. If you choose to reenter a relationship with the wrongdoer, then that individual must change."

Wil provided the following insight on forgiveness:

Each situation that causes pain, physical or emotional, can either strengthen or weaken your spirit. Of course, we, your spiritual guides, hope you choose to move forward with strength, understanding, and forgiveness. We welcome the opportunity to help you. If you desire insight into your problem, ask. Pray for help if you get stuck. You can either be left in the chains of the past or free yourself to shape your future through forgiveness. Look at each new day as an empty canvas. You may fill it and make changes in any way you choose. If you wake up in the morning with painful baggage from years, months, or even the day before, take the time to clear the issue. You deserve to live in peace. You also deserve an exciting life filled with a positive attitude, new opportunities, and wonderful experiences. Go in peace.

11. BE OPEN TO RECEIVE INFORMATION. UNDERSTAND THAT YOUR ABILITY TO RECEIVE INFORMATION CLEARLY CAN AND WILL CHANGE FROM DAY TO DAY.

Welcome the opportunity to communicate with your guides. The quality and depth of your connection will vary based on whether you desire the communication. But it's also all right if you just don't feel like connecting. Sometimes weeks pass during which I don't have any conversations with Wil regarding personal issues. But even if you decide not to connect, for whatever reason, keep the lines of communication open through your willingness to receive.

Don't be concerned if your connection with your guides is stronger one week than another. This is normal and could be the result of changes in your mood, feelings, or preoccupations. Lack of communication means not that you have lost the ability to connect with your guides, but that you are fully occupied with other pursuits. For instance, I became preoccupied for a month in planning a friend's bridal shower, acting as matron of honor, and assisting in any way I could with her wedding preparations. I barely connected with Wil during that time.

Connection is not a competition. How much time you spend communicating with your guides or the length of the messages you receive is not important. Furthermore, connection will not be taken away as "punishment" for wrongdoing, but you must seek to recognize your mistakes and ask forgiveness. Remember, connection is to be used to help yourself, others, and the world. The how, what, where, and when will depend on your own life's purpose.

12. PRACTICE. YOUR ABILITY TO COMMUNICATE WITH YOUR GUIDES WILL IMPROVE.

Besides strengthening your ability to connect, practice will help you determine the approach that is most suitable for you. One woman devoted fifteen minutes every day to asking questions and writing down the answers from her guides. After a month or so, she was able to communicate without writing down the questions first. She was thrilled to learn that she could receive the answers anytime, anyplace. When she did write in her journal, however, as she continued to do from time to time, her answers were more complete and she could review them.

Another student of mine tried to write down her responses but did not like the process. After the first few questions, she preferred to listen for the answers to come into her thoughts. Sometimes, however, when she felt the answers needed clarification, she would write down a paraphrase of her guides' messages and ask if she had written it correctly. This can be a successful technique for practicing connection.

If you receive your messages through images, you need to practice so that the images are as clear as possible and you can interpret them correctly in words to yourself and others. Practice improves visual communicators' ability to receive messages in images and also, curiously, auditorily. This is quite an advantage, because auditory messages can add meaning to images, diminishing your need to interpret them. Kinesthetic communicators cannot rely completely on receiving messages through feelings, because feelings alone may not give a detailed enough idea of what is being communicated. I recommend that kinesthetes also learn to receive messages visually, auditorily, or both. If you experience a feeling when communicating with your guides, make a note of it and then get further information by asking for auditory or visual responses.

Regardless of your communication style with your guides, practice is the only way for you to improve your skills.

13. YOU DO NOT NEED TO PROVE YOUR ABILITY TO CONNECT. KNOWING IN YOUR HEART THAT YOU CONNECT IS SUFFICIENT.

Since the purpose of this gift is to help yourself and others, your motivation to connect must be based on love. If someone tries to test your ability to connect by asking you the name of Aunt Mildred's cat, it may be best not to try to get an answer. You could say, "I would be happy to help you resolve an issue, but I don't feel comfortable using this gift just to prove that connection exists. Would you like to ask another question?"

Your questioner may try to test you again, and you can choose whether to proceed. This may be a perfect opportunity to help an open-minded skeptic. But if you are still uncomfortable, tell the person, "Let's try another time." You do not need to explain yourself further.

14. DO AND ASK ONLY WHAT IS COMFORTABLE FOR YOU.

You are in control. You have the freedom to choose what you do, and if you feel uneasy with something, do not do it or reveal it. I once tried to help a woman who had a hostile attitude. As our conversation progressed, I found myself on the defensive. Squirming in my seat, I wondered how I could end the discussion. I decided to ask Wil for guidance instead, and he recommended that I ask the woman what was upsetting her. This question made her stop and think, and put an end to her challenging of me. It transformed the situation, and we ended the evening on a positive note.

15. YOU HAVE THE FREE WILL TO CHOOSE WHAT YOU DO WITH THE GUIDANCE YOU RECEIVE.

When your guides provide you with information, it is always to help you or someone else. You have the free will to ignore their guidance, although the consequences may not always be what you would wish. A woman I taught named Nora told me the following story that clearly illustrates this point. Every day a man in Nora's neighborhood walked his dog near her home. Nora lives on a very busy street, and often this man would come over and talk to Nora and her children as their dogs roughhoused together. One day Nora and her children were outside when she saw the man and his dog approaching from a distance. At that very moment, she received a clear and direct message to grab her dog, gather up her children, and go into the house. Though the message was strong, she couldn't see why she should follow it. Besides, the man had already spotted her and waved. How could she go into her house without seeming to snub him? Not wanting to be rude, she stood with an uneasy feeling as he approached. The message was repeated, yet she couldn't bring herself to act on it.

When the man was close enough, he took his dog off its leash as he had often done before and let it cross the street. As the dog bounded across the road, a car came whizzing around the corner and struck the dog, which sustained near-fatal injuries. After extensive treatment, the dog recovered fully, but Nora has always greatly regretted ignoring that message. This is a dramatic example, but whenever you are able to take immediate action, you ought to do so.

16. REMEMBER TO BE APPRECIATIVE.

Thank God and your spiritual guides for the opportunity to connect and for the information you receive, for their helpful guidance and gift.

CHAPTER 8

IT'S TIME TO
CONNECT

Now that you have a basic understanding of what connection is about, have determined your principal mode of communication, and have studied the guidelines, it's time to put what you've learned into practice. I'll begin by showing you some examples of how to frame your questions and remain open to your guides' answers, then move on to procedures for connection based on whether you are an auditory, visual, or kinesthetic communicator. Review the guidelines after you have practiced connecting using the techniques in this chapter, and periodically thereafter as you feel the need.

HOW TO FRAME A QUESTION FOR YOUR GUIDES

When I teach workshops on connection, I divide the class into groups of four to eight people who do not know one another. I then give each person an opportunity to ask a question on which he or she would like everyone in the group to receive information. You can try to frame your questions on your own or with one to three friends.

1. Make your question clear, brief, neutral, and to the point. Do not give any details that would lead listeners to a conclusion or an answer you would prefer to hear. If you are asking the question by yourself, frame it as neutrally as possible. Ask it in the first person and make the question open-ended, beginning with a phrase such as "What do I need to know about _____?" rather than "Should I _____?"

A man named Paul who was attending one of my workshops for the first time was deeply troubled by the fact that the house he had been renting had been sold and he had only sixty days to find a new place to live. He had been shown several houses that didn't much appeal to him, but he felt he ought to take one because he was running out of time. Rather than have him ask "Should I rent such-and-such a house?" I suggested he phrase his question this way: "What do I need to know about finding a new place to live?"

When Paul framed his question that way, he received a number of surprising answers. One suggested that he get in his car and drive, turning left, then right, then left, then right again, until he came to the right house for him. He interpreted this to mean that he should relax about the process and look at many houses, knowing that the right one would present itself within the allotted time, which is what happened. Paul and his family are now extremely happy with their new house, and Paul is convinced that had he taken one of the others out of desperation, he would have been very disappointed in the long run.

2. When you receive answers from your guides, get as much detail as possible. Do not be afraid to ask for further information and verification if necessary.

These instructions clear the way for members of the group to recognize the messages they receive from their guides. Most people will accept whatever comes to them and write it down to share. The majority receive similar messages, and saying the answers aloud and hearing their similarity allows the group to recognize that the messages came from a higher source—"strangers" could not possibly know the information disclosed. Here's an example.

MARA'S QUESTION: What can Mara do to enhance her present relationship with her partner?

MESSAGE 1: Passion! Pour on the passion. Do not hold back. Give in to the love.

MESSAGE 2: Make love more often. Making love will bring out the desire on his part to care for you and make you happier.

MESSAGE 3: Mara needs to talk more, share more. Be open, write love letters, and love will start flowing from you to him.

MESSAGE 4: Don't be so anxious; relax and enjoy.

MESSAGE 5: Sing and dance (together). Try more fun ideas.

MARA'S RESPONSE: Wow! These messages were right on the money. My partner is very sexual. He needs a lot of love, and I now realize that sex is a part of his need to be loved. He's also a very sensitive person. I used to think that his need for sex was selfish, but these messages helped me recognize that his needs are legitimate. His response is always very loving and positive, and he shows me the love that I need right back. I am naturally very serious and reserved, and I have a great deal of trouble relaxing. I find it difficult to enjoy the moment because I'm always analyzing everything in our relationship. Now I understand that when I'm playful he's playful too, and we have a lot of fun together. He takes my lead on most things, and I need to make an effort to have fun with him.

The message "write love letters" is incredible. That's how we got to know each other. We haven't written love notes in years. He's a real card person, and even though we lived in the same town, we loved writing back and forth. It really added a spark to our relationship. I'm definitely going to start writing those notes again.

AARON'S QUESTION: What can Aaron say to his father and what can he do for him?

MESSAGE 1: Keep doing what you have been doing. You're a good son, just keep being a good son. Your devotion is already making an impact on lives other than yours and your dad's.

MESSAGE 2: Be honest. Tell the truth. Say all those things you wanted to say and clean the slate both ways. Share wounds and joys. Love and appreciate each other. Hold with support. Do what you already are doing, and we'll do the rest. You'll help him into the light.

MESSAGE 3: Tell him you love him and that it's OK for him to move forward [into the light]. Tell him that you are all grown up now and willing to let him go on—if that is what he chooses. Tell him you know it's his choice now and you won't stand in his way. Make him as comfortable as possible and touch him as much as possible: massage or rub his forehead, his earlobes, and feet. Spend time with him alone, hold him. His leaving has nothing to do with you. It's time for him to move forward. He will be OK.

MESSAGE 4: Tell him you love him. Let him be comfortable. Help him feel good. Nutrition!

MESSAGE 5: Aaron, nature is taking its course. It is important that your father be comfortable. Make sure his comfort needs are taken care of. Say it all—everything your heart desires without sadness [past regrets are not necessary]. Your father understands you better than you think. Your admiration of this man is commendable. But he is still just a man. Let his last days be of comfort. And be at peace, for your father can always be with you and you can seek him out for guidance.

MESSAGE 6: Be with him. Reminisce. Laugh! Humor!

MESSAGE 7: [This was a visual image that required

Aaron's interpretation.] I see Walt Disney–type characters try-ing to open a window that is stuck. They're trying to get out.

AARON'S RESPONSE: All of these messages make sense to me. My dad's been very ill and doesn't have long to live. The Disney characters are very interesting. My father always enjoyed humorous, lighthearted char-acters. He's a funny person who enjoys telling jokes and laughing with people. The stuck window symbolizes my dad's need to get out. He's been held in restraints, and I think that image shows his feelings of being tied down and his desire to move on. Of all my dad's children, I've always felt that I would be the one to help him go to the light. These messages confirm this for me. It's interest-ing that someone mentioned massage. The last time I saw my father, I massaged his feet and he loved it. It seemed to bring him a lot of comfort. Several people talked about making my father comfortable, and mas-sage seems to be one way I can help him. I'm also going to spend some time with him and let him know how I feel. I've always admired this man.

The next day, a woman in Aaron's group called him. She told Aaron she had received a message that his fa-ther would enjoy fresh-squeezed juice. It seemed like a strange message, but she decided to pass it on anyway. The next time Aaron visited his father, he brought fruit and a juicer. It turned out to be the best thing he could have done for his dad, who was thrilled, enjoying every last drop of juice. Aaron said it actually brought some sparkle back into his dad's eyes. Since the initial meet-ing, Aaron has received calls from other participants with messages to pass on to him. Those messages continue to help Aaron with his father's impending death.

During one of my workshops, in response to a question from a participant, I received a rather lengthy message. I knew nothing of the person about whom he was asking, nor what type of relationship existed between them. Notice how his question was very general, yet the answer from the guides direct and clear.

JOEL'S QUESTION: What's the best path for Joel regarding Marianne?

MESSAGE: Joel, it is best for you to open your heart to her and speak your mind. When you approach her with a loving honesty, you will reflect the essence of being lovingly truthful. Marianne needs acceptance. You can give this to her without being dishonest about your feelings. Marianne is a caring person who can sometimes brush people the wrong way. This is a protective coat she wears to keep herself safe from what she perceives as a threat. On the other hand, she strives to have acceptance and greatly needs it! Lay out your intentions for her like this: "I care about you and want to discuss an important matter." Make her feel safe so that the conversation can be open and honest, not hostile and closed. Your approach can be the difference between walking on eggshells and smooth sailing. Go for what you believe is right.

It is best that you have your objective points clear in your mind. Write them down. This way you have set your goals for the conversation. Marianne's greatest need right now is support. You can give it without compromising what you truly believe is right! That is all now. Be at peace.

JOEL'S RESPONSE: This message provided insight

and gave me a clear approach in handling my relationship with Marianne. I've been dating her for only a few weeks, and I realized that even though I enjoy being with her, it's difficult for me to see any future with her other than a friendship. Marianne is quite a bit older than I am and had just come off a difficult breakup when I met her. This left her feeling vulnerable, and she seeks a great deal of support and acceptance from me. Her need for support is the key to this whole situation. It's why I feel that I'm withdrawing from her. She's having a difficult time with male-female relationships, and she demands a great deal of support, much more than I feel I can give to her now. I truly believe that she needs me more as a friend than a boyfriend. And I'd like to be just that—a friend.

Marianne does wear a protective coat, especially when you first meet her. She canceled our first two dates because she was afraid to get hurt. It took a while for her warmth to come through. She really does need acceptance, and I'm concerned about how she's going to handle our conversation. I know she's terrified of being rejected. I realize that I must be careful in my approach but still be truthful.

As important as it is to learn to frame questions for your guides, it's even more essential that you learn to accept their answers after verifying them, even when their messages are unexpected or unusual. My neighbor Marie and her friend came over one Saturday to learn how to connect with their guides. Marie was going that afternoon to a weeklong pottery seminar, but she wanted to learn spiritual communication before she left. As I instructed them, my children constantly interrupted. I was also expecting my relatives to arrive shortly, so I uncharacteristically rushed through the information. I provided the basics and prayed that Marie and her friend would successfully connect with their guides. Marie received some information in response to a question and then asked for her guides' names. Sitting at my kitchen table, her eyes closed as she tried to block out the noise around her, she suddenly smiled and started to laugh. "I'm getting the name Bob," she said. "What kind of name is Bob for a guide? Could this possibly be correct?"

I confirmed that Bob's name was correct. Marie then told me that she could see what he looked like. "He has long, dark hair and wears it in a ponytail. He's tall and thin, and I think he wears an earring. Wow, what a description for a guide! He's a real cool guy."

As my family arrived, I informed Marie that Bob would be with her only for the duration of the pottery seminar. I said that he was not a very advanced guide but she would learn from him. That was all. When Marie arrived home a week later, she was bursting with excitement as she relayed what had happened during the seminar.

"I arrived late," she said, "and everyone was already in the cafeteria eating dinner. After I got my tray, I went to the only seat left in the room and sat down. I asked the man across from me if I'd missed anything. He said that I hadn't, and then added, 'By the way, my name is Bob.' When I heard the name, I took a closer look at him.

My jaw dropped, and I had to look away. He was the exact image of the guide I'd described earlier that day. I was shocked because I never thought Bob would turn out to be a real person. During the course of the week, I realized that I would have avoided him altogether because he looked intimidating with that long ponytail and the earring. But I decided to put his appearance aside, and we spent the week talking to each other about life. I learned quite a bit about pottery from him, too. He turned out to be an extraordinary person.

"I still can't get over it. One word, *Bob,* and a description of his appearance changed the whole course of my week. Who would ever have guessed it?"

I asked Marie if she thought she'd see Bob again.

"No, I don't think so," she replied. "I think we were meant to cross paths only for that short time. But what a time it was!"

To this day, Marie has had no other contact with Bob.

Sometimes I'm tempted to dismiss a message when it seems totally off the wall or makes me uncomfortable. The next example illustrates this point. At one of my workshops, a woman named Terri asked for guidance regarding her business, and the answer I received from her guides had an unexpected ending.

TERRI'S QUESTION: What can Terri do to help make her business successful?

MESSAGE: Explore avenues for growth. Look in the Yellow Pages and check to see what businesses you can possibly approach to expand your sales. Stay positive. Know that you have the skills and the know-how to run a business and that you do not need to fear failure. You can succeed. If you feel you've taken a lump, don't let it cloud your vision. You know what you want. Achieve it! By the way, nice thighs!

TERRI'S RESPONSE: She immediately burst into laughter. "I can't believe it! What you don't know is that I just lost thirty-five pounds. Only a few hours ago, I told a friend that even though I had lost all this weight, I would always have thunder thighs. I can't tell you how happy this makes me feel. Thank you, thank you!"

The rest of the information was helpful, but that last line had the strongest impact on Terri's life. And I was glad I didn't give in to the temptation to ignore a part of the message that seemed both odd and irrelevant to the question.

Asking questions properly and remaining open to whatever answers you receive are prerequisites for receiving accurate information. Now, according to your dominant mode of communication, choose the section appropriate for you and follow the steps I've outlined.

HOW TO CONNECT IF YOU ARE AN AUDITORY COMMUNICATOR

Since auditory communicators prefer to hear instructions, you may want to tape-record the following directions and then replay each step. Otherwise, read them aloud once and then go back to the beginning to get started. You can also have someone else read them to you.

1. Sit quietly in a comfortable chair or at a table with your journal and pen. Peace and quiet are important for your concentration. With time and practice, you may be able to ignore noise and receive information even in a loud place.

2. State either aloud or in your thoughts, "I am open, willing, and ready to receive information from my highest spiritual guides. My guides communicate with me out of love and light." (However, you may connect with only one guide.)

3. State and visualize if you can, "I am surrounded by love and light."

4. Think of an unanswered question that you would like to ask your guides. You may ask a yes or no question, but in any case, frame it neutrally.

5. Clear your mind of any personal thoughts you may have about the question to allow the information from your guides to come through.

6. Write your question in your journal. As you do so, say the words aloud or to yourself.

7. As you finish writing, be ready to receive the answer immediately. You may get the answer before you complete the question, almost like taking dictation.

8. If you believe you are thinking instead of receiving information from your guides, or nothing immediately comes to you, then occupy your mind by restating the question either aloud or in your mind repeatedly until you hear the answer within your thoughts. This will keep your mind focused on the

question instead of on your thoughts. Be patient. The message will come.

9. When you have received the information, write it down as you received it.

10. Read over the information you recorded. Write and ask, "Did I correctly write the information I received?" Listen for a yes or a no answer. You may also rephrase the question: "Have I received the correct information?" Or "Did I write the answer correctly?" If the answer is yes, proceed with another question or the next step. If the answer is no, say the original question over and over again, either aloud or to yourself, until you receive the answer. Or ask your guides, "What do I need to know?"

11. If the answer you wrote is brief and you would like additional information, write and say, "Please elaborate on _____" or "Please give me more information about _____."

12. If you do not understand your message, say so in writing. Ask for more information or an explanation.

13. Ask again, "Did I receive and write the information correctly?" Listen for a yes or a no. If the answer is no, request more information.

14. Write and say, "Is there anything else I need to know about _____?" Listen for a yes or a no. If the answer is yes, ask by writing the question, "What is it?" Again, write the message as you hear it or as the words form within your thoughts.

15. Before you end, ask for your guides' names. This

will help you to establish a relationship and allow you to initiate communication with your guides in the future.

16. Thank your guides for the information you received.

HOW TO CONNECT IF YOU ARE A VISUAL COMMUNICATOR

If you are a visual communicator, you should read all the instructions first, then go back and reread each one as you go through the process. You may want to close your eyes after each step to help you "see" images.

1. Sit quietly in a comfortable chair or at a table with your journal and pen. Peace and quiet are important for your concentration. With time and practice, you may be able to ignore noise and receive information even in a loud place, but start out by finding a sanctuary in which your connection can occur.

2. Visualize and state either aloud or in your thoughts, "I am open, willing, and ready to receive information from my highest spiritual guides. My guides communicate with me out of love and light." Write a description of any image that comes when you say these words. Be aware that you may connect with only one guide.

3. State and visualize, "I am surrounded by love and

light." You may want to close your eyes to do this. Then write a description of any images that come to you.

4. Try to visualize your spiritual guides. Trust whatever images come to you. Write your description in your journal.

5. Think of or visualize an unanswered question that you would like to ask your guides. You may ask a yes or no question, but in any case, frame it neutrally.

6. Clear your mind of any personal thoughts you may have about the question to allow the information from your guides to come through.

7. Write your question in your journal. When you are through, read it several times. Then close your eyes and picture the question in your mind.

8. As you finish writing, be ready to receive the answer immediately. You may get the answer before you complete the question. Write down whatever comes to you. Remember, the answer may come in the form of visual images, so you may need to close your eyes to receive the message.

9. If you believe you are thinking instead of receiving information from your guides, or nothing immediately comes to you, then occupy your mind by visualizing or rereading the question repeatedly. This will keep your mind focused on the question instead of on your thoughts. Be patient. The message will come.

10. When you have received the information, write it down as you received it.

11. Read over the information you recorded. Write and ask, "Did I correctly describe the information I received?" Wait for a yes or a no image. You may also rephrase the question: "Have I received the correct information?" Or "Did I write the answer correctly?" If the answer is yes, proceed with another question or the next step. If the answer is no, reread and visualize your original question over and over again until you receive the answer. Or ask your guides, "What do I need to know?"

12. If the answer you wrote is brief and you would like additional information, write and visualize, "Please elaborate on _____" or "Please give me more information about _____."

13. If you do not understand your message, say so in writing. Ask for more information or an explanation. (Note: Some visual communicators may receive verbal messages from their guides in addition to images.)

14. Ask again, "Did I correctly write the information I received?" Wait for a yes or a no image. If the answer is no, request more information.

15. Write, "Is there anything else I need to know about _____?" Wait for a yes or a no image. If the answer is yes, write, "What is it?" Again, write the message as the images form in your mind.

16. Before you end, ask for your guides' names. This will help you to establish a relationship and allow you to initiate communication with your guides in the future. Be aware that it may be difficult to receive names if your messages are all visual.

17. Thank your guides for the information you received.

HOW TO CONNECT IF YOU ARE A KINESTHETIC COMMUNICATOR

Kinesthetic communicators sometimes need to do something physical to help them communicate with their guides. This may be as simple as writing down the information. Some find walking around or gently tapping their feet helpful. As you process information kinesthetically, you may feel sensations in your body. It is common for strong sensations to surface. Keep in mind that these physical or emotional sensations convey important messages from your guides. For example, if you ask a question about a family member and you experience a sensation that you relate to joy, then determine how this feeling may correspond to your question. On the rare occasion when you may experience a strong sensation such as pain, overwhelming sadness, frustration, or loneliness, I recommend that you acknowledge it but then say that you want it to go away. If you feel a pain in your shoulder, for instance, say, "I recognize this pain, and I want it to leave now." If you get a profoundly sad feeling, say, "I understand there's some sadness associated with this question, but I don't need to feel it personally." Then ask your guides to explain in words or images why you experienced that pain or feeling. To help yourself let go of the pain or strong feeling, think about or visualize something joyous, or take a few deep breaths. Suffering need not be part of the connection.

Kinesthetes may find it useful to read Eugene Gendlin's book *Focusing,* on how to refine their "felt sense" of intuitions and experiences.

Since it may be difficult for you to receive all the information you need from your guides by kinesthetic means (touch, internal and external feelings), the steps that follow incorporate auditory and visual techniques.

1. Sit quietly in a comfortable chair or at a table with your journal and pen. If you feel the need to walk around or gently tap your foot, do so. Peace and quiet are important for your concentration. With time and practice, you may be able to ignore noise and receive information even in a loud place, but start out by finding a sanctuary in which your connection can occur.

2. State, "I am open, willing, and ready to receive information from my highest spiritual guides. My guides communicate with me out of love and light." Describe in your journal how these words make you feel. Be aware that you may connect with only one guide.

3. State, "I am surrounded by love and light." Again, describe how the love and light feel to you.

4. Describe any feelings you may have that you associate with connecting with your guides.

5. Think or visualize an unanswered question that you would like to ask your guides. You may ask a

yes or no question, but in any case, frame it neutrally.

6. Clear your mind of any personal thoughts you may have about the question to allow the information from your guides to come through.

7. Write your question in your journal.

8. As you finish writing, be ready to receive the answer immediately. You may get the answer before you complete the question. Write down anything that comes into your thoughts, describe any images you receive, and observe carefully how your body reacts and where you feel any change of emotion, any heaviness or lightness or movement in your body.

9. If you believe you are thinking instead of receiving information from your guides, or nothing immediately comes to you, then occupy your mind by retracing or rewriting the question repeatedly. This will keep your mind focused on the question instead of on your thoughts. Be patient. The message will come.

10. When you have received the information, write it down as you received it.

11. Read over the information you recorded. Write and ask, "Did I correctly describe the information I received?" Listen for or visualize a yes or no answer. You may also rephrase the question: "Have I received the correct information?" or "Did I write the answer correctly?" You may even experience a physical response that you will be able to correlate to a yes or a no answer. For instance, you may

sense tingling or the flicker of a finger for an affirmative answer. Once you recognize your signal, it will be reliable for you. If the answer is yes, proceed with another question or the next step. If the answer is no, write your original question over and over again until you receive the answer. Or ask your guides, "What do I need to know?"

12. If the answer you wrote is brief and you would like additional information, say and write, "Please elaborate on _____" or "Please give me more information about _____."

13. If you do not understand your message, say so in writing. Ask for more information or an explanation.

14. Ask again, "Did I correctly write the information I received?" Listen, watch, or observe your physical reactions for a yes or a no. If the answer is no, request more information.

15. Write, "Is there anything else I need to know about _____?" Listen for a yes or a no, wait for a visual image, or observe your physical reaction. If the answer is yes, write, "What is it?" Again, write the response you hear, see, or feel in your journal.

16. Before you end, ask for your guides' names. This will help you to establish a relationship and allow you to initiate communication with your guides in the future. Do not be concerned if a name does not come to you right away, especially if your messages come to you visually.

17. Thank your guides for the information you received.

ADDITIONAL TECHNIQUES TO ENHANCE YOUR ABILITY TO CONNECT

1. Learn connection with a friend. Get together and exchange questions. Try to give each other questions that you couldn't answer on your own. Then each of you sit quietly and proceed with the communication mode that suits you best. Write down whatever images or words come to you. Remember, do not interpret or question the information. The message is intended for your partner and may very well make no sense to you, but your friend will understand it. After you both finish writing something down, share the messages.

2. If you followed all these instructions but still seem to have difficulty receiving answers from your guides, try this technique, which I have found quite successful. Have a friend repeat a question aloud ten times or more as you sit quietly with your pen and paper. Since you will be busy listening to your friend's voice, you will be less likely to "think" of an answer. As your friend repeats the question, write down whatever comes to you. Closing your eyes may help you to concentrate or receive an image. If you do not have a friend to help you, record the question on a tape recorder fifteen or twenty times. An answer may even come to you while you're recording the question. If it does not, replay the tape and focus on your voice. Write down whatever comes to you.

IF YOU'VE DONE EVERYTHING AND STILL CANNOT CONNECT WITH YOUR GUIDES

Wil advises, Your guides are with you and anticipate your connection. Do not give up. You will communicate with your guides.

Certain preconceived attitudes or mind-sets may initially cause you difficulty in connecting with your guides. The most potent takes the form of a negative belief: "I'm not going to be able to do this." Yes, you can. There is nothing magical about connecting, but beliefs and feelings like this block your ability to receive. Be positive and expect that you can and will communicate with your guides. State until you are comfortable, "I am open, willing, and ready to receive."

You may need to change your communication mode. If you attempted to connect with your guides auditorily without success, try the instructions for the visual or kinesthetic methods.

Another common stumbling block is too much thinking or analyzing: "Every time I write down a question, I start thinking of the answer." "It's difficult for me to shut out my own thoughts." "I question if this could possibly be right." Don't get frustrated. Reread the previous section of this chapter. These simple methods are helpful when you are thinking or analyzing the answers to your questions.

Perhaps most frustrating of all is when nothing comes to you: "My mind's blank. I've tried to be open, but I'm not getting anything." People who make this comment are usually very good at clearing their thoughts and anticipating a response from their guides. But for some reason either they blocked a response to their questions or a word came to them but was quickly dismissed with statements such as "It's my own thought" or "This doesn't make any sense." By rejecting the word or words you receive, you can block additional information from coming through. Even if the answer is obvious or is one that you are not happy about having received it may still be good, relevant, or spiritual guidance. If, indeed, nothing came to you, then try another communication mode.

Finally, an unresolved barrier issue may make it difficult to connect with your guides. This issue may influence your life to the point where it is difficult for you to free yourself from negative emotions that in turn affect your ability to connect. Read the following chapter about barrier issues, and, if you identify a troublesome issue, think about ways to resolve your problem. One option is to pray to God for help. Be patient; the answer will come to you. Another alternative is to say sincerely, "I am open to guidance. Please help me resolve my issues." This may very well be the catalyst for you to receive guidance.

One morning I was extremely crabby and knew my mood related to a childhood issue I had to address. I needed help but did not feel like connecting with my guides. Instead, I prayed for the answer to come. An hour later, my sister called. Since she lives far away, we don't speak as often as we would like. She wasn't calling for any particular reason, and when we were about to hang up, I felt compelled to discuss my thoughts and feelings about the past. She knew just what to say to help me, and as I listened to her soothing and insightful words, I realized that she was the answer to my prayer.

If you still have difficulty connecting with your guides, go to the self-help section of your bookstore and silently ask to be guided to a book that will help you the most. Then examine any book that draws your attention. The assistance you need may well be found within those pages. I recommend *You Can Heal Your Life* by Louise Hay, but there are plenty of other books that may be able to help you. Your body can also help you clear problems through alternative healing techniques such as Reiki, acupuncture, and kinesiology. You may want to investigate these to find out if one works for you. Finally, consider spiritual counseling, support groups, or other professional help. Remember that your goal is to seek truth in order to have a peaceful and loving existence.

IF YOU LOSE THE CONNECTION YOU HAVE ESTABLISHED

It is perfectly natural for communication with your guides to increase or decrease at different times. Don't think that your guides have left you or that you have permanently lost your ability to communicate with them. Continue to ask your questions with the realization that the answers may come to you from another source, such as a friend or neighbor, the newspaper or television. Our guides recognize that answers sometimes need to come through others or by experience. Be open to these options and know that it is likely that your guides had a part in leading you to the answer. If you ask questions for several weeks and there is still no communication, examine whether you are blocking your connection because you're not sure that you really want answers or even to communicate with your guides. They will respect your decision and allow you to live your life as you choose. When you desire to connect, state with a sincere heart, "I am ready and want to connect again."

Negative feelings and how we view ourselves can interfere with connection, but we do not lose connection as punishment for something we have done. The gift of forgiveness from others and within ourselves will have a tremendous impact on our ability to connect. Recognize that you have the choice to remain stuck or move forward.

If, with open mind and heart, you've followed the instructions and suggestions contained in this chapter and the guidelines described earlier and have still been unable to connect, don't despair. It's more than likely that a barrier issue of some sort is blocking your ability to communicate with your guides. Pay close attention to the next chapter and you will probably find out what is holding you back.

CHAPTER 9

THE FIVE BARRIERS TO CONNECTING WITH YOUR SPIRITUAL GUIDES

At times, we all confront barriers to our spiritual advancement, and this is certainly true of connecting with our guides. The issue is never the existence of barriers but how we deal with them.

There are five major barriers that can hinder an individual's ability to connect with spiritual guides, Wil explained. They are lack of faith, fear, feelings of unworthiness, lack of trust, and self-centeredness.

Once you are aware of your barriers, you can address the issues in your life that contribute to them. For instance, the faith you lack could be faith in the benevolence of the universe or faith in your own abilities. The issue that is setting up a fear barrier could be your fear of violence because you have experienced it. Your feelings of unworthiness could revolve around low self-esteem rooted in childhood abuse. You do not have to resolve all your problems in order to connect with your guides. You must be willing, however, to make positive changes, to move forward in your life.

On one occasion, for instance, I had been in a bad mood for a week. Unfortunately, I had no idea why I felt so out-of-sorts and I had no desire to talk to Wil, so we did not communicate. I finally decided to get rid of my gloomy attitude by asking Wil for insight. He referred to a conversation I'd had with an acquaintance who had unknowingly roused my belief in my own unworthiness so that I had become depressed.

> You really don't want the pain, Liza, Wil said, but when you experience it, your sadness reinforces your feelings of not being worthy and your lack of desire to take care of yourself. You can stand on your own two feet. Your identity does not lie within your mother. She is a separate being. Yes, you came forth from her, but your birth was God's gift. Make the absolute most of that gift. We tell you this out of love to help you see. Open your eyes and mind to see what we see: a bright, capable woman. We wonder why you question your God-given strengths and qualities. Open your heart to yourself, my dear. God bless you and be with you always.

This message made me aware of how much I allowed others to influence my self-esteem and helped me begin to move beyond that harmful habit.

It may sound self-evident, but the first step in resolving barrier issues is learning to identify them. Your guides can help you. Simply say, "I know something is holding me back, but I have no idea what it is. Can you please help me to understand?" If you are upset, you may need to relax to allow the information to come through. If you have difficulty communicating with your guides because you are distressed, wait until you are in bed or alone to relax and concentrate.

We all desire to feel good. If, however, you choose to feel good by avoiding your barrier issues or denying your feelings, the problems surrounding them will continue to cause you frustration, concern, or distress. Facing problems is sometimes painful, but the pain will pass when the problem is resolved. Remember that you are never alone; your guides are always there to help you, even if you don't connect with them consciously. Let them help bring peace to your troubled mind.

As you read the following sections, if you feel drawn to one, pay particular attention to it. Each section contains some ways to begin working through a barrier. You may, of course, identify more than one barrier in your life, but choose the one that most closely explains how you react to situations on a daily basis or the one that needs the most immediate attention.

LACK OF FAITH

Wil explained, Lack of faith in yourself, others, or God is the first reason why it may be difficult for you to connect with your spiritual guides. Furthermore, some people do not believe spiritual communication is possible. A spiritual relationship comes to each individual within his or her own heart. It cannot be forced upon someone. Do not use the gift of connection to prove its existence to nonbelievers. Rather, use it to improve your life, to help others, and to make the world a better place.

A student of mine named Rita tried to explain her experience of connection to her skeptical husband. He insisted that there must be another explanation. She desperately wanted his approval of her newfound spiritual connection and her renewed faith in a Higher Power, yet he could not give it. Several times she asked questions concerning her husband's life to "show" him that connection is real. He would not confirm any of the answers she received, even though they were correct. When she shared her personal experiences, her husband shook his head in disbelief. Rita continued to communicate with her guides and stopped trying to persuade her husband. As connection became a natural process for her, as her own life improved and her relationships with people around them improved, her husband gradually began to accept its existence.

Even after you have established communication with your guides, doubt and disbelief can impede connection. If you say to yourself, "This information could not have come from my guides, it must have come from me," then you create doubt in your mind.

The following questions can help you determine if lack of faith is your barrier issue:

+ Do you doubt the existence of a Higher Power?

+ In general, are you skeptical of spiritual existence?

+ Do you feel it's pointless to pray?

+ Do you doubt your ability to make good decisions?

+ Do you question whether others can help you get
the job done?

+ Did a tragedy destroy your faith?

If you answered yes to most of these questions, then
lack of faith is probably an issue for you. If that's the
case and you desire spiritual connection, begin with
prayer. Any words you use to ask for guidance will be
appropriate, as will any of the following affirmations. If
you struggle with faith, your renewed spiritual journey
is just beginning. God bless you. Be patient with yourself as you find faith.

These affirmations may help you with lack of faith,
or doubt:

I am open to God's wondrous works.

I accept what I receive as God's gift and message for
me.

It is OK for me to believe and accept that connection exists.

I have faith in myself to _____.
(Example: "I have faith in myself to know I received spiritual guidance.")

Wil's Message

If you doubt the existence of spiritual connection, then we ask you to seek the truth of our existence. Information on receiving spiritual guidance is documented in the Bible, in a variety of books, and even on some television shows. Please be willing to give us the opportunity to help you. Open yourself to the possibility of spiritual guidance. We welcome your questions, even when you do not connect directly with us. We will do whatever we can to guide you to information. Be open to receive. We look forward to helping you.

Once you connect, we ask you to have faith in us. We will always speak the truth to you out of deep love. Know that our purpose is to help, that is all. Go in peace, and God bless you.

FEAR

Most individuals fear the unknown, the intangible, or unfamiliar people and places, cultures and concepts. If you fear communicating with spiritual guides and if

you react to life in a fearful manner, then it is not surprising that you have a barrier to connection. You will
need to confront and work through your fear.

Wil explained,

Though it's dramatic for us to appear in physical form
to reach people, it is usually not necessary. When we
develop an ongoing communicative relationship with
you as a "spiritual teammate," we will have a more positive effect on your life. We can always communicate
effectively with you by thoughts, images, or feelings.
Once connection becomes commonplace, your fear
will subside or disappear.

Your beliefs about the devil or evil can create fear.
Fear itself holds you back, not any evil force. When you
know that we are with you out of a pure, deep, and
profound love, and that we support you in your life's
journey, then your fear of communication with your
guides will diminish.

Our purpose is to inspire, teach, and encourage
you—not to make your life more difficult but to make it
better. We will help you grow and bring you closer to
your Higher Power. Realize, however, that you have
free will and the ability to make decisions. It is always
your choice to establish and develop a relationship
with us. You will never hear us say that you must,
should, or should not do something. Our advice is for
guidance. What you do with it will be your decision.

Sometimes a fearful reaction lets you know that
something is wrong. You may want to stop and listen be-

cause it is often a symptom or signal of negative beliefs. If you examine why you are afraid and learn from the experience, fear will not paralyze you. Unfortunately, people frequently get stuck behind their fear, which prevents them from accomplishing what they desire in life.

One of my workshop students told me about a family member who disliked her dead-end job. The woman prayed for a job opportunity to come her way, and sure enough it did. She accepted a position with another company, but as she prepared her resignation, fear started to take over. Miserable as she was with her current employer, at least she knew her job well. What if the new position were worse or she didn't get along with her new boss or coworkers? In the end, she turned down the job offer. How unfortunate that she saw only negative possibilities. Her fear clouded her ability to accept change.

Fear can control your decisions, but your quest for truth, love, and understanding will prevent fear from dominating your actions. You have nothing to fear except what you create in your mind. You always have other choices, but when fear guides your decisions, you close yourself off from them.

I once met a woman with a phenomenal ability to heal her illnesses and injuries. "The process is very simple," she said. "Anyone can do it." Yet she thought that if she shared her abilities with others, she might lose them. I tried to get her to examine this negative belief and suggested that if she taught others or cured sick people, her gift might actually expand. Why would God punish a generous act of healing and sharing by diminishing her own health or ability if she acted out of faith and humility? She quickly dismissed my suggestions. I believe that unless she can see past her fears, she will stunt her own healing potential and spiritual growth.

The following questions can help you determine if fear is your barrier issue:

+ Are you afraid of change?

+ Do you look at the negative possibilities instead of the positive ones?

+ Are you an excessive worrier?

+ Are you afraid to make decisions and prefer others to make them?

+ Does fear dictate your life?

If you answered yes to most of these questions, then fear is your barrier. Awareness is the first step to overcoming fear. Next, identify situations in your life that cause you to react with fear. Write down everything you believe could go wrong and why you are afraid. Now write all the positive possibilities on a separate piece of paper. Destroy your negative list, then reread your positive list and post it somewhere in your home for review. Do not put yourself down if you feel afraid. Acknowledge your fearful thoughts and change them to positive ones.

These affirmations may help you with fear:

I am safe and secure and surrounded by God's love and light.

I am open to seeing new possibilities in my life.

I view life positively and make good decisions.

I am open, willing, and ready to receive helpful information from my spiritual guides.

Wil's Message

Fear not, dear ones. We watch over you and are with you. Let us provide helpful guidance. See a different view of your world, one without fear of the negative possibilities. We cannot always keep you from pain, but we will ease your way. Know that we deeply love you and that you are surrounded by the love of God.

FEELINGS OF UNWORTHINESS

Wil explained, When you feel unworthy of connection with us, you put a barrier in place. A relationship with us is not contingent on being a perfect person. Instead, it is based on your desire to help yourself, others, and the world. We will give you the words of encouragement to help you overcome this barrier.

If you feel unworthy of love, attention, happiness, or success, your self-image is generated not from within but from how you believe others perceive you. Often, even though you do your best to succeed, you unfairly criticize yourself. These criticisms will destroy a part of your self-esteem, and you will want to work on replacing your negative thoughts with kinder attitudes toward yourself.

As a schoolteacher, I see children rip up or throw away their work because "it just wasn't good enough." These students often need more time to finish their assignments because they are afraid to make mistakes. Some of them will verbally devalue their work even after I've praised it. I try hard to help these students understand that mistakes are a natural part of life and most often an excellent opportunity to learn.

Ask yourself, "Was I this way as a child?" Your adult feelings of unworthiness correlate to childhood events. If you consistently give more than you receive from others, your need to give indicates your lack of self-worth, and you must develop the ability to receive love and appreciation. According to the Quality Life Training seminars of Tom Mahas, an expert on personal development, we can compare giving and receiving with breathing in and out. It is as impossible only to breathe out as it is to believe that we should only give and never receive. By allowing others to give back, you help them experience the in-and-out breath of life. Practice giving yourself love and compassion. Be open and gracious about accepting what others, including your guides, have to offer.

The following questions can help you determine if feelings of unworthiness are your barrier issue:

✦ Does constructive criticism hurt your feelings?

✦ Do you seek approval or recognition from others?

✦ Is it difficult for you to accept a compliment, even though inside you rejoice?

✦ Do your sensitivity and need for approval control your interactions with others?

✦ Do you constantly compare yourself with others and conclude that others are better than you?

✦ Do you gossip to make yourself feel better?

If you answered yes to most of these questions, then take a moment to ask yourself, "Why do I feel unworthy?" It may be time to address your feelings and make a conscious effort to change.

To resolve the issue that lies at the bottom of your unworthiness, identify an event that hurt your self-esteem, then replay the scenario in your mind. Allow yourself to feel the anger, hurt, pain, or sadness. Acknowledge the feelings until you are ready to release them. How would you want to react differently if given another chance? Imagine or talk your way through the experience again, but this time change the outcome. Remember, your intention must never be to hurt anyone, even with your thoughts. Once your changes are complete, you will react differently if faced with the same challenge. Finally, choose to stop beating yourself up for previous "mistakes." Your negativity will not change the past. Decide to regain control over your life. You deserve to be happy.

I spent all of my childhood and part of my adult life determined to get my mother's approval, and I relied heavily on what she said and did to establish whether I was worthy of love, friendships, success, and happiness. I finally decided to stop giving her or anyone else the power to control my sense of worth. Now I rely on what comes from within.

As with all the barriers to connection, feelings of unworthiness recur even after you have dealt with them once or several times. Each time you face a familiar troubling situation that activates one of your barriers, your guides will help you work through it more quickly and with a lot less pain. Don't be discouraged if barriers don't crumble immediately—they took a long time to build. Once you have begun to work through them, however, you will see your power increase as the power of your barriers to stop you decreases.

These affirmations may help you overcome your feelings of unworthiness:

I am worthy of connection with my spiritual guides.

I forgive myself for _____, and I allow myself to move forward out of love and peace.

I respect and love myself exactly the way I am.

I approve of myself.

I learn from my past mistakes and release them.

I am worthy to receive _____, have _____, participate in _____.

When you say, "I forgive myself" or "I am worthy to receive _____," specify the issue or situation that is most significant to you. For example, "I forgive myself for not being patient with my children, and I allow myself to move forward out of love and peace."

Wil's Message

Nothing you have done will keep you from deserving our spiritual guidance. Even if you have broken God's laws, repentance opens you to God's guidance. Remember that our mission is to help you with your God-given life purpose. When you seek help, we are there for you. Be open to our guidance and do not worry, you are worthy. God bless you on your journey.

LACK OF TRUST

Wil explained, When you connect, lack of trust can be a problem, because you question whether you received correct information from us. You may say, "Well, I know this is what I heard, but is it correct?" You can always ask for clarification or additional information from us. Eventually you will come to trust your answers.

Anna found it very difficult to trust her messages. After she learned to connect, she called me each time she received information to verify its accuracy. She was right on target, yet she was racked with doubt. A few weeks later, her guides instructed me to stop establishing the credibility of her messages. She needed to trust herself and her guides. I passed on their message, and Anna agreed to work on trusting the information. It was difficult to say no when she asked me to confirm "just one thing," but I did. In time she learned to trust the insightful information from her guides.

Answer the following questions to help determine if lack of trust is your barrier:

✦ After you complete a task, do you worry about whether you did it correctly?

✦ Is it hard for you to trust your decisions?

✦ Do you question the motives of others?

✦ Was there an occurrence in your life that destroyed your trust of others or your ability to be trusted?

✦ Did someone chronically lie to you?

✦ Are you a chronic liar?

+ Did someone betray your trust?

+ Do you prefer to do things yourself because it is hard for you to trust others to do them right?

If you answered yes to most of these questions, it may be difficult for you to trust or be trusted. Decide to leave the past behind and look deep within to understand why you have problems trusting yourself or others. Stop carrying the burdens of the past into each new day.

A close friend of mine—I'll call her Lauren—had a serious problem trusting her second husband. Each time he left town on business she worried that he might have an affair, even though he'd done nothing to indicate he was unfaithful. As she worked on this problem with her guides, they led her to examine how she interacts with other people in general, especially female friends and family members. She came to see that she was questioning everyone's motives for actions as innocent as turning down her dinner invitation because of a previous engagement. Over time Lauren recognized that her lack of trust had developed when her first husband left her for another woman, so she worked on leaving the past behind and enjoying a trusting relationship with her new husband—and everyone else around her.

To help yourself build trust, you must address why it is so difficult for you to trust others. Write your reasons down. Allow yourself to feel the pain, anger, and resentment they call up. Tell yourself, "I am in control of my life. Though _____ hurt me, I choose to move on. The past will not hold me back now that I understand why it was so difficult for me to trust others. I can forgive _____. I deserve to be happy."

Rip up the paper and throw it away. Now list and post your goals to help you trust again. Each morning when you get up, read them. Do the same just before you go to sleep. You can trust.

If you were untrustworthy in the past, how do you want to rebuild trustworthiness? To forgive yourself, you must understand why you behaved deceitfully. Think of an incident in which you let someone down or destroyed another's trust. Write out what happened, including the result. Ask yourself, "Why did I need to destroy _____'s trust in me?" Perhaps behind your dishonest behavior are feelings of unworthiness. If you are unsure and do not connect, pray for the answer to come. It will. With understanding and loving-kindness, forgive yourself and, if possible, ask the person you have hurt to forgive you. Then allow yourself to move on with a new outlook. Write and post your goals to help you regain the trust of others and of yourself. Read them in the morning and just before you go to sleep. You can be trusted.

These affirmations may help you build trust:

I am a trustworthy person (in my relationships, with my family, in business, and so on).

I trust myself enough to know that I receive correct information from my guides.

I trust myself and know my guides provide helpful information for me and others.

I allow myself to release the past. I no longer need to carry the burden of _____ (fill in trust issue).

Wil's Message

Trust us, dear ones. We will always speak the truth to you. Know that the more you connect, the more you will trust us. When you open your heart to trusting others, you will realize how integrated you are with them. Your inability to trust can separate you from others. A life of trust is more enjoyable than one of mistrust and deceit. Look at your world differently. Allow yourself to start with trust instead of distrust. Know that there are people who are worthy of your trust. Forgive those who have wronged you. God bless you on your journey.

SELF-CENTEREDNESS

The final barrier to connection is self-centeredness. Wil explained, You will not successfully communicate with us if your purpose in connecting is to control or be superior to others. Your motivation to connect must come from your heart, out of a desire to help yourself, others, and the world, without any selfish intentions.

Answer the following questions to help you see whether self-centeredness is your barrier:

✦ Is it extremely important to you to be better than everyone else?

✦ Do you hate to lose at anything?

✦ Do you get angry or work ten times harder if others surpass you?

✦ Do you spend time cutting others down to feel important?

✦ Do you compare what you have with what others possess and strive to possess more than the next person?

✦ Do you dismiss others' opinions when they are different from your own?

✦ Does constructive criticism make you irate?

✦ When you give, do you expect something in return?

After you have answered these questions honestly, reflect on your past. Perhaps you will be able to see what triggered your egocentric focus. When you identify the reason for it, you may be able to release the need to have life revolve around you. As you begin allowing yourself to enjoy the flow of life, you will no longer require the protective shield of superiority that you constructed. The desire to control everything within and outside your grasp will begin to fade away.

The following questions may help you pinpoint the start of your self-centeredness:

+ Can you think of incidents in your childhood when you were put down by others?

+ If you were not the best, were you perceived as a failure?

+ Were possessions overly important to you or your family?

+ Were you noticed or praised only when you surpassed others?

As with all the previous barriers, the key to overcoming self-centeredness is identifying it. Once you are aware of how you react to others, you can choose to change. Take some time to forgive those who have hurt you, and realize that they, too, have issues. Financial or career success is fine as long as it is not the most important thing in your life and you do not sacrifice relationships in order to "win." You can push people aside for only so long before you end up alone.

After you identify this issue and connect with your

guides, ask for their help to overcome your self-centeredness. Their guidance will provide opportunities for opening your heart and soul to others. When you give unselfishly, the rewards surpass any personal satisfaction you may have achieved from acting egocentrically.

These affirmations may help you with the barrier of self-centeredness:

I recognize and acknowledge the value in others.

I am open to others' ideas.

The words I speak are positive and helpful.

I willingly give up my need to control others, and I encourage their endeavors through my actions and words.

My best is good enough, even when others surpass me.

Wil's Message

You have many God-given talents and gifts. When others benefit even more than you from these skills, you serve God. Be true to yourself, but know that you must serve others. Share your talents. You can give in many ways by keeping your ego in check. When you connect, be willing to open your heart to the guidance we

have to offer you. We will lead you in your path to helping others. God bless you.

Barrier issues clearly create problems in our lives
that it would be helpful for us to resolve even aside
from learning to connect. As part of the process of identifying and resolving these issues, you may find it helpful to have a specific goal. Most people, when asked
what they need to do after defining a problem, will respond, "Find a solution." But if you do not define your
goal first, you'll never obtain a solution. How can you
help a person who is lost (his or her problem) until you
know where that person desires to go (his or her goal)?

Wil explained, We will help direct you in a way that will
lead to the identification of your goals. It is imperative, however, that you ultimately determine your own goals because we
will not interfere with the choices you make. If you ask us
"What do I need to do with my life?" we will offer possible directions and options that reflect your strengths.

Once you desire to understand and resolve problems, the following model, provided by Tom Mahas in
his Quality Life Training seminars, may prove effective
and helpful:

1. Identify and define the problem.
2. Set your goal or goals.
3. List possible solutions.
4. Take action.

Your guides will offer possible solutions if you need
them. In many situations, once you identify your prob-

lem and set your goal, the solutions will flow. If you need help with finding solutions, say to your guides, "I don't know what my options are. Can you help me identify them?" They will assist you. They will also help you identify which option may represent a better direction to take. But your guides will never say that you must or should follow a particular path. You are the only one who can put into action the solution you have chosen. Your guides can encourage you to maintain the motivation necessary to fulfill your goal, but that motivation must come from within.

Even after identifying and resolving any problems or barrier issues and achieving your goal of connection, however, you may find that once in a while a message you receive seems to be incorrect. This does not mean that the whole process is flawed. In fact, it can be explained by a variety of reasons that we will explore in the next and final chapter.

CHAPTER 10

CAN THE INFORMATION I RECEIVE APPEAR TO BE INCORRECT?

When I started to communicate with Wil, I was excited and gratified by my ability to convey his information to family and friends and help them. There were times, however, when I realized that the message I had delivered was off the mark. When that happened, I found myself questioning my ability to receive information at all. I often asked myself, "What went wrong?" I felt embarrassed that I had delivered incorrect messages when my avowed purpose was to be helpful. "How could I have botched the message?" I would ask Wil.

First, Wil explained, the information we receive from our guides is always correct. Several issues or situations can arise, however, that may lead to an "incorrect" understanding of the information: You may have interfered with the answer through a judgmental attitude or misunderstood it. You may have cut off communication too soon or misinterpretated your guides' messages. I'll explain these problems and others in this chapter.

1. YOU MISINTERPRETED THE INFORMATION OR MADE ASSUMPTIONS.

It is all too easy to read between the lines when you receive information from your guides. But you should realize that the assumptions and interpretations you make can be wrong. If you receive answers from your guides visually, it is important to be aware of your interpretations and ask for verification if you are unsure. If you receive auditory messages, your guides mean exactly what they say. Ask for verification if you don't understand their precise meaning.

For example, one evening I received a strong auditory message for Eric, a close relative. His guides said, "Soon Eric will be offered a new position at work."

"I knew it," he responded when I passed the message along to him. "I don't know why, but I just knew it."

"Wait," I said. "I'm getting a job description." It perfectly matched Eric's talents and skills. I was overjoyed for him, and in my excitement I made an assumption that the job described by his guides would be the job offered, even though his guides never indicated this. The next day Eric was offered a new position, but not the one I described. When he called, I could hear the disappointment in his voice. "I don't understand it," he said. "This new position is a horrible match for my skills. I can't figure out why they offered it to me and why you were told something totally different."

I desperately wanted to answer his questions, but I was too distraught to connect with Wil. Instead, I sought clarification of what had happened from some of the people I had taught to connect. Their insight was extraordinarily helpful. One person told me that the job Eric was offered was an honor that validated his hard work and accomplishments at the company. Another student explained that Eric's guides had described the ideal position for him because the timing was perfect for Eric to present it to his superior. If he chose to, Eric could explain to his boss how the proposed position would serve the company and utilize his talents.

After hearing my students' input, Eric decided to approach his manager, state his goals, and define his skills. If nothing else, his boss was impressed with Eric's initiative. Perhaps the message I received was meant to indicate that Eric needed to be clear about his own skills and future.

This episode taught me about how an assumption can lead to a wrong conclusion. Remember, the information from our guides is pure. Be careful not to manipulate the message through your interpretations.

2. YOU CUT OFF COMMUNICATION TOO SOON.

When you break the connection with your guides, either because you don't want to hear the message or because you jumped to a conclusion, you shut out their guidance. One day I asked Wil, "Is there anything I need to know?"

Yes, I heard. Justin's morning may be rough. I didn't want to hear that, so I cut off communication. Doubting Wil's words, I concluded that I must have misunderstood. Fifteen minutes later, when it was time for Justin to get on the bus, he burst into tears. He did not want to go to school. I later realized that if I had allowed Wil to continue, I would have been prepared to help Justin. Instead, my beliefs interfered with Wil's communication. This situation reminded me that our guides provide information only to help us; they don't give us apparently troubling messages just to make us feel bad. Avoid conclusions and allow yourself to receive the information.

3. YOUR PERSONAL BELIEF IS CONTRARY TO THE TRUTH.

Wil explained, Your guides will not interfere with your truth, even when that truth is incorrect, because we respect your free will to choose your beliefs. If you ask a question, however, we will present the truth. For example, if you believe the sky is green, it is green. But if you ask your guides whether the sky is green, the answer will alter your truth.

Be aware that your guides may lead you to experiences that will positively affect what you believe. For instance, I always thought of myself as someone who did not judge people. I now realize that at times I did make judgments and hold on to them. Those judgments may have prevented me from getting to know people better or acting always out of kindness and compassion. Wil explained, You are given the ability to make judgments, and, therefore, you have no reason to feel ashamed. If you hold on to your judgments, however, you close off other possibilities. Be willing to let go of your initial judgments.

Sometimes you may receive information that will force you to take a hard look at yourself or others. Perhaps the information does not fit your current belief systems, making it difficult for you to be objective. Do not be distressed. Remember to write down the message and ask your guides for insight. Or put the message aside. You may understand the message at a later date, when you can examine the situation more realistically. There have been times when I had difficulty accepting information from my guides because I was not ready for it. This was perfectly all right. In all these cases, I eventually comprehended the validity of the message and resolved the issue. Do not change or make a decision unless you are ready to do so. Do not alter the information to fit your beliefs. When you are ready to reexamine the situation, your guides will be waiting with loving insight.

4. YOUR QUESTION WAS NOT FOR A HIGHER GOOD. THEREFORE, THE ANSWER WILL NOT BENEFIT ANYONE. IN THIS CASE, YOUR RESPONSE WILL ALWAYS BE NO.

Wil explained, The questions you ask must come from your heart, out of a desire to help yourself, others, and the world. No other motivation is acceptable. Your questions will not be answered if their purpose or results are not for a higher good.

5. YOU HAD DIFFICULTY LISTENING OR YOU'RE NOT CERTAIN YOU HEARD CORRECTLY.

If you had difficulty listening to a message or are not certain you heard it correctly, repeat the question or ask for clarification. Restate what you heard or describe the image or feeling you received and then ask if it was correct. If you are still unsure, repeat the question, or let some time pass and try again. One of my students related that it was very difficult for her to connect with her guides when she tried to do more than one thing. Interruptions were frustrating, and she received only bits and pieces of information. She was most successful when she sat quietly, with no distractions. Some people can immediately tune out noise and connect, even in a busy place. Others need a quiet spot to communicate with their guides. With practice, your ability to receive your guides' messages will improve.

6. YOU FEEL UNSURE OF YOURSELF AND ARE UNCERTAIN OF YOUR CONNECTION WITH YOUR GUIDES.

The more you connect, the more you build confidence in your ability to receive helpful guidance. If your messages seem jumbled and you wonder about their accuracy even after receiving confirmation from your guides, say the following affirmation to build faith and trust in yourself and your guides: "I am open, ready, and willing to receive information from my guides. I am able to accept and recognize their messages." If this problem persists, you may want to review the sections in Chapter 9 on barriers arising from lack of faith or trust.

7. YOU FEAR THE TRUTH, SO YOU RECEIVE WHAT YOU WANT TO RECEIVE. YOU MAY FEEL SECURE FOR THE MOMENT, BUT YOU MUST WORK THROUGH THE FEAR.

Wil explained, Sometimes it is scary to examine a situation that you need to deal with. So instead of receiving our guidance, you listen to your own thoughts and shut ours out. Eventually you will have to work through the issue. Please do not shy away from confronting your problems. We love you and want to help you.

When you have a negative attitude about an issue

in your life, your spiritual guides may have a difficult time communicating with you. You can become so engrossed in your problem that you aren't receptive to their guidance. When you finally do ask for advice but still are not quite ready to receive it, you may interject your own beliefs into the message or cancel the information completely. In these cases, you may have to address another, more serious reason to regain peace—most likely a barrier issue. When you are ready, examine the issue and put it aside.

8. YOU ASKED THE WRONG QUESTION. YOU RECEIVED THE INFORMATION FOR THE QUESTION ASKED, BUT WHAT YOU MEANT TO ASK OR WHAT YOU NEEDED TO KNOW WAS ENTIRELY DIFFERENT.

Wil explained, Your guides will answer your question. We do not interpret whether you meant to ask something else.

One time, after receiving guidance, I waited too long to write the message down. By the time I did, I had garbled it and it no longer made much sense. I asked Wil, "Did I receive the information correctly?" I heard Yes, but what I ought to have asked was, "Did I *write* the information correctly?" I would have received the response no. I later realized that I received the message correctly but, because I waited to write it down, I transcribed it incorrectly.

9. YOUR NEGATIVE THOUGHTS INTERFERED WITH YOUR GUIDE'S COMMUNICATION.

Any negative, judgmental, or unkind answers to your questions may very well be your own beliefs coming through. In such a case, you haven't really connected. If the message reflects your beliefs, recognize that it most likely came from within. For example, my friend Anna went through a period when everything she seemed to receive was negative: "Your name is babyish. You need to lose a few pounds." She realized that these thoughts directly reflected her negative self-image. Once she recognized this, she worked through the barrier issues, and such words ceased to come up again.

Now that you have examined the reasons information can appear to be incorrect, you are fully prepared to connect successfully with your guides. I encourage you to review this section periodically along with other chapters in this book. Doing so will help to keep the information fresh in your mind and can serve as a catalyst for communication with your guides.

Although some years have passed since Wil's early September morning appearance, I can assure you that I am still in awe of this process. I continue to struggle with old issues from time to time, but I am able to deal with challenges more easily and quickly now because of the valuable insight my guides lovingly provide. Even if our lives and the world around us sometimes seem to be out of control, our guides are constant in their willingness to help us help ourselves, others, and the world. As you ask for their assistance, be aware of the positive changes in your life; watch how guidance has a subtle and perhaps even profound influence on people around you. You are beginning a wondrous journey. I hope that you, too, will see yourself as a person who can utilize the gift of spiritual guidance to change your life in many ways.

CONNECTION IN ACTION

What a joy it is to wake up with no expectations yet find that, by the end of the day, my life has been utterly transformed by the spiritual guidance I've received during the day. The first time this happened to me, it completely changed how I view myself and others. And, further, my guided actions positively influenced most of the people with whom I came in contact in the course of the day.

Early one morning as I lay in bed waiting for my children to get up, I suddenly heard Wil suggest an excursion to the zoo. "That's a great idea," I responded. "The kids will love to see the animals. Thank you."

Why don't you ask your friend Anna to go with you? Wil added. I looked at the clock. It was 8:00 A.M., and without getting out of bed, I picked up the phone and called her. Anna was delighted by Wil's suggestion. "Sounds wonderful," she said. "Let me get the boys ready, and we'll meet around ten o'clock."

When we arrived at the zoo, Anna looked a bit flustered. "I almost called you to cancel because the boys were really demanding this morning," she said. "I asked my guides if they thought it was a good idea for us to come to the zoo, and I heard yes. I hope it turns out to be a good day."

It almost didn't. Ten minutes into viewing the animals, Wil told me that I had left my wallet on top of my car. Anna watched the children as I ran back to the parking lot. Arriving out of breath, I saw the wallet in plain view, exactly where Wil had said it would be. I checked its contents and was relieved to find that everything was there. I thanked Wil and was buoyed by a renewed belief that the world is still filled with good people who do not take advantage of others.

When I returned, Anna pointed to a man with a long ponytail and a red bandanna on his head. Just a minute before, her son had shouted, "Hey, Mom, there's a pirate!" We both laughed as she related the incident. Her son was a fan of Captain Hook, and when the man glanced over at us I explained why we were laughing. He smiled, and though he didn't say anything I sensed something special about him.

As we walked around the zoo, we repeatedly saw this man and his daughter. We didn't converse but did exchange grins. "If I see him one more time," I told Anna, "I'm going to tell him that he has a really nice aura."

Tell him if he works hard in his endeavors, Wil added, he will be successful in life.

I thought, Why not? You never know how a simple statement can change a person's life forever. I agreed to repeat the message if I saw the man again.

By then it was time for lunch. We had planned to leave, but in the spirit of the moment we decided to eat at the zoo cafeteria. I promised my elder son that I would buy him a souvenir, so Anna and I agreed to meet in the dining area. After we made our purchase, the kids and I walked into the restaurant. As I approached the counter, I noticed a homeless man. He had shaggy, shoulder-length hair, a beard, a long coat, and baggy pants, and he obviously hadn't bathed for a while. Instead of being repulsed, I sensed something extraordinary about him. When I sat down at the table with the kids, I said to Anna, nodding toward the homeless man, "I just asked God to watch over him."

"Me, too," she said. "How do you think he got into the zoo?"

"He paid, of course," I responded as if I knew.

I decided to take action. I realized that I could not live with myself if I didn't help him in some way. Without a word, I opened my wallet and took out some money. I wondered how I could give it to him without insulting or embarrassing him. Scanning the room, I spied the napkin dispenser. That's it, I thought. I'll wrap the money in a napkin.

The homeless man stood up and began to walk away

slowly. I seized the opportunity and confidently approached him with my gift in hand. "Here," I said, "this is for you."

He took it and began slowly unwrapping the napkin. "What is it?" he asked.

"God bless you," I whispered shyly.

"I *hope* so," he said.

"I know so," I answered.

By now he had unwrapped the napkin and discovered the money. "Oh, *thank* you," he said. "May I give you a hug?"

"Sure."

He embraced me with tender strength, then pointed to the glass door. "Are you going out?"

"No, we're done for the day," I said and paused, unsure of what to say next. We stared at each other, smiling. "Well, take care," I said, and with a wave he turned and walked away. As I made my way to the table, I looked back and he was gone.

When I sat down, Anna said, "I can't believe you did that. Weren't you scared?"

Gripped with emotion, I shook my head. Tears streamed down my face. After I composed myself, I explained. "I'm not crying because of his predicament. He'll be OK. I'm crying because he gave me so much more than I gave him. He gave me his greatest possession—his love."

Shaking my head, I added, "I should have given him more." Wil entered my thoughts: It's OK, Liza. It's OK. You saw the beauty of a person's soul. You did just fine.

I felt at peace. I knew that I had learned some valuable lessons and set an example for anyone who saw my actions. This experience fortified my faith and reinforced my joy in giving and receiving. I realized I could never again hold on to a judgment without stepping into the other person's shoes. I began to look deeper to see other people's inner beauty. This event changed my life in the same profound way that giving birth had. Both experiences altered my definition of who I am.

As we prepared to leave, I saw the man we had fondly nicknamed the Pirate walk into the gift shop with his daughter. "Would you keep an eye on the kids?" I asked Anna. "I'll be right back."

She nodded. I went into the store and found the man kneeling next to the T-shirts. I stopped in front of him and exclaimed, "I know this may sound strange, but I wanted you to know that you have a beautiful aura, and if you work hard in your endeavors you'll be successful."

Looking up at me with a broad smile, he said, "Thank you."

"You're welcome," I responded. I quickly turned and left the store.

When I returned, Anna asked, "Did you buy something?"

"No," I said. "I just fulfilled my promise and gave the Pirate his message."

As I drove off, I saw the Pirate and his daughter exit the zoo. It was a beautiful ending to a miraculous day.

The experiences Anna and I shared that day with each other, our children, the Pirate, and the homeless man made a lasting impression on both of us. Not every spiritual communication with your guides will be as momentous as that day was for Anna and me. I have found, however, that such experiences have a cumulative effect; every communication is a chance to help myself or others. The help we seek may be for a friend who has lost her car keys or for ourselves to understand and resolve our problems. Regardless of whether we see an issue as big or small, our guides rejoice in helping us help ourselves and others.

As you advance on your path of personal development, take the knowledge you gain from your spiritual guides and make this world a better place for you and the generations to come.

GUIDELINES FOR QUICK REFERENCE

1. Keep a journal.
2. Be a clear and direct communicator.
3. If in doubt, ask for confirmation of what you received.
4. Speak the truth.
5. If you receive information about someone and you are unsure whether you should reveal it, always ask. If you feel uncomfortable with the information, do not repeat it. You have the right to choose what you share.
6. Remember that information is confidential.
7. Understand that connection is a gift.
8. Connection is to be used for spiritual growth. Use what is revealed to you only for good, out of deep love, to help yourself, others, and the world.
9. Be patient with yourself and others.
10. Forgive yourself and others for shortcomings. Work on your own improvements.

11. Be open to receive information. Understand that your ability to receive information clearly can and will change from day to day.
12. Practice. Your ability to communicate with your guides will improve.
13. You do not need to prove your ability to connect. Knowing in your heart that you connect is sufficient.
14. Do and ask only what is comfortable for you.
15. You have the free will to choose what you do with the guidance you receive.
16. Remember to be appreciative.

A P P E N D I X 2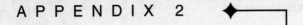

JOURNAL
BEGINNINGS

DATE: _____ TIME: _____ QUESTION: _____
SAMPLE QUESTION: WHAT DO I NEED TO KNOW TODAY?

_____

_____

_____

_____

_____

_____

_____

DATE: _____ TIME: _____ QUESTION: _____
SAMPLE QUESTION: WHAT INSIGHT ABOUT _____
(A PERSON) CAN YOU, MY HIGHEST SPIRITUAL GUIDES,
PROVIDE ME TO IMPROVE OUR RELATIONSHIP?

_____

_____

_____

_____

_____

_____

_____

_____

_____

_____

_____

_____

DATE: _____ TIME: _____ QUESTION:_____
SAMPLE QUESTION: WHAT INSIGHT CAN YOU, MY
HIGHEST SPIRITUAL GUIDES, PROVIDE ME ABOUT MY
JOB?

_____

_____

_____

_____

_____

_____

_____

_____

_____

_____

_____

DATE: _____ TIME: _____ QUESTION: _____

_____

_____

_____

_____

_____

_____

_____

_____

_____

_____

_____

_____

_____

BIBLIOGRAPHY

Castelli, Jim, ed. *How I Pray: People of Different Religions Share with Us That Most Sacred and Intimate Act of Faith.* New York: Ballantine, 1994.

Daniel, Alma, Timothy Wyllie, and Andrew Ramer. *Ask Your Angels.* New York: Ballantine, 1992.

Dossey, Larry, M.D. *Prayer Is Good Medicine: How to Reap the Healing Benefits of Prayer.* San Francisco: HarperSanFrancisco, 1996.

———. *Healing Words: The Power of Prayer and the Practice of Medicine.* San Francisco: HarperSanFrancisco, 1993.

Fagan Dzelzkalns, Lee Ann. *View from the Mountaintop: A Journey into Wholeness.* Milwaukee, Wis.: Ageless Dominion Publishing, 1995.

Hay, Louise. *You Can Heal Your Life.* Carlsbad, Calif.: Hay House, 1987.

Gendlin, Eugene T., Ph.D. *Focusing: A Step-by-Step Technique That Takes You Past Getting in Touch with Your Feelings to Change Them and Solve Your Personal Problems.* New York: Everest House, 1979.

Kaplan, Aryeh. *Jewish Meditation: A Practical Guide.* New York: Schocken, 1985.

Kushner, Rabbi Harold S. *When Bad Things Happen to Good People*. New York: Schocken, 1989.

Mark, Barbara, and Trudy Griswold. *Angelspeake, a Guide: How to Talk with Your Angels*. New York: Simon & Schuster, 1995.

Occhiogrosso, Peter. *The Joy of Sects: A Spirited Guide to the World's Religious Traditions*. New York: Image Books, 1995.

Roman, Sanaya, and Duane Packer. *Opening to Channel: How to Connect with Your Guide*. Tiburon, Calif.: H. J. Kramer, Inc., 1987.

Scholem, Gershom. *Kabbalah*. New York: Meridian, 1978.

———. *Major Trends in Jewish Mysticism*. New York: Schocken Books, 1988.

Shapiro, Rabbi Rami. *Wisdom of the Jewish Sages: A Modern Reading of Pirke Avot*. New York: Bell Tower, 1993.

INDEX

messages in, 50–51, 53–54,
  62, 89
misinterpretation in, 144
statements about, 64–65
visualization, 43
voice, inner, 14–15, 43

welcome, from Wil, 17–19
white lies, 74–75
Wiemer, Liza M.
  and Crohn's disease, 30–32
  initial connection with Wil
    and, 1–16, 22
  life history of, 22–32
  parents of, *see* father;
    mother
Wil
  childhood communications
    with, 23–24

on faith, 124
on fear, 125, 128
and higher guides, 7
initial connection with,
  1–16, 22
message to the reader from,
  17–19
and negativity, 3, 5
physical manifestation of,
  3, 5
on self-centeredness,
  139–40
on unworthiness, 128, 132
wisdom, embodiment of,
  14–15

yoga, 60

zoo, excursion to, 153–58

ABOUT THE AUTHOR

Liza M. Wiemer has taught in a religious school for the past fourteen years. She has served as president of the Milwaukee Temple Youth Group and as president of the Northern Federation of Temple Youth. She currently teaches seminars to adults based on the information contained in this book. Liza (pronounced "Leeza") lives with her husband, Jim, and her sons, Justin and Evan, in Milwaukee, Wisconsin.

You can contact Liza M. Wiemer at

P.O. Box 23408
Milwaukee, WI 53223-0408

or by e-mail at

jlwiemer@aol.com.

She is interested in hearing from readers who have stories about how connection has improved or affected in any way their life or the life of someone they know.